Advance Praise for *Plug-in* ___

Sherry Boschert does a great job of showing how shifting to hybrid plug-in cars can sharply reduce gasoline use, dependence on imported oil, and carbon emissions. If we simultaneously build thousands of wind farms across the country, feeding cheap electricity into the grid, we can then run our cars on wind energy — and at a gasoline equivalent price of less than $1 per gallon. What are we waiting for?

— LESTER R. BROWN, President, Earth Policy Institute, and author of *Plan B 2.0: Rescuing a Planet Under Stress and a Civilization in Trouble*

This is an important book. As a historian I was intrigued by the history; as a reader I was charmed by the writing; as a citizen I was outraged by the auto industry's duplicity. If you think your car should get a few more MPG (like 30 more!), plug into *Plug-in Hybrids*. It will recharge your political batteries.

— MARTIN SHERWIN, Pulitzer Prize winning author of *American Prometheus: The Triumph and Tragedy of J. Robert Oppenheimer*, and professor of history, Tufts University

Plug-in Hybrids is a must-read. If you are concerned about the environment, national security, or high gas prices, there is a solution and it's contained in this book. But this isn't simply a book about cars, it's a book about our future. And our future started to look brighter with every page I turned. I was riveted!

— ALEXANDRA PAUL, EV driver and actress

An informative, provocative, engaging book about a vital topic, *Plug-in Hybrids* is an important book for the 21st century.

— OCEAN ROBBINS, Founder and Director,
Youth for Environmental Sanity (YES!)

Today's efficient hybrids are just a starting point for pioneers who desire ultra clean, far higher mileage vehicles. *Plug-in Hybrids* documents the beginning of a cleaner environment and security for all.
Our future is watching, is this race on?

— DR. JACK MARTIN, Sustainable Transportation, Appalachian State University vice-chair, Renewable Fuels and Transportation Division, American Solar Energy Association

Plug-in Hybrids

THE CARS THAT WILL RECHARGE AMERICA

Sherry Boschert

NEW SOCIETY PUBLISHERS

CATALOGING IN PUBLICATION DATA:
A catalog record for this publication is available from
the National Library of Canada.

Cover design/digital composite by Diane McIntosh.
Image "Divine Nature," iStock: Eric Taylor. Photodisc: Stormy Sky.

Printed in Canada.
First printing September 2006.

Paperback ISBN 13: 978-0-86571-571-8
Paperback ISBN 10: 0-86571-571-4

Inquiries regarding requests to reprint all or part of *Plug-in Hybrids*
should be addressed to New Society Publishers at the address below.
To order directly from the publishers, please call toll-free (North America)
1-800-567-6772, or order online at www.newsociety.com

Any other inquiries can be directed by mail to:
New Society Publishers
P.O. Box 189, Gabriola Island, BC, Canada V0R 1X0
1-800-567-6772

New Society Publishers' mission is to publish books that contribute in fundamental ways to building an ecologically sustainable and just society, and to do so with
the least possible impact on the environment, in a manner that models this vision.
We are committed to doing this not just through education, but through action.
We are acting on our commitment to the world's remaining ancient forests by
phasing out our paper supply from ancient forests worldwide. This book is one
step toward ending global deforestation and climate change. It is printed on acid-
free paper that is 100% old growth forest-free (100% post-consumer recycled),
processed chlorine free, and printed with vegetable-based, low-VOC inks. For
further information, or to browse our full list of books and purchase securely, visit
our website at www.newsociety.com

NEW SOCIETY PUBLISHERS   www.newsociety.com

To Meg and to Barbara

With love and gratitude

CONTENTS

Introduction

PERSONAL TRANSPORTATION in North America depends almost entirely on petroleum. The freedom that cars, light trucks, and sport utility vehicles (SUVs) give us comes with a price. These gasoline vehicles produce more than a third of the greenhouse gases that come from the United States and add to global warming. The need for gasoline leaves our economy at the mercy of other oil-producing nations, many of whom don't particularly like us.

Something's got to change if we're to avoid the crises that lie squarely ahead of us because of this situation — political crises, climate volatility, ecological devastation, economic hardship, and military conflicts.

One solution — the plug-in hybrid — has caught the imaginations of all kinds of people who normally wouldn't agree on much of anything else. A politically polarized America is coming together over plug-in hybrids. Why? Because plug-in hybrids will save drivers money, cut pollution and greenhouse gas emissions, and improve national security by reducing our dependence on imported petroleum.

This book explains what plug-in hybrids are, why people want them, and what you can do to get one. Plug-in hybrids get plugged into a regular wall socket at night to recharge the batteries while the driver sleeps; their engines supplement the electricity with gasoline or biofuel for long-distance driving. The cost of fueling is less than half what you'd spend to drive a regular hybrid, and plug-in hybrids reduce greenhouse gas emissions by half.

Although you can't yet walk in to a car dealer and plunk down a deposit for a plug-in hybrid, they're likely to be available soon. Your actions can help bring them to market sooner.

I began longing for a car that runs on electricity after my family put solar panels on our home in 1998. With clean electricity coming from the sun, an electric car seemed the next logical step. We've since had two electric cars made by major auto companies and loved them both. I haven't been to a gasoline station in years. By driving on electricity, I've spared the world more than 2 tons (1.8 metric tons) of global-warming emissions from the car alone, not counting the emissions reductions from our solar panels, which replace electricity from polluting power plants.

Yet now I'm excited about an electric car that *does* have a fuel tank — the plug-in hybrid — because I understand that all-electric cars have some limitations, and most Americans are not ready for them yet. Plug-in hybrids overcome those limitations while still bringing most of the benefits of electric cars in saving fuel and reducing pollution. I'm also convinced that once people become familiar with plug-in hybrids, they'll feel comfortable driving electric cars.

The story of plug-in hybrids necessarily includes the stories of both electric cars and of conventional, gasoline-dependent hybrids, because they show us not just where plug-in hybrids came from but why our actions are important for plug-in hybrids to succeed. Chapter 1 describes how auto and oil companies tried to suppress electric cars and plug-in hybrids in the late 1990s and early 2000s, and why they gave us hybrids instead.

Many Americans, if they think about electric vehicles at all, probably think of them as a flop; a perception that is understandable but incorrect. Courageous California State regulators forced the major car companies to create zero-emission electric vehicles in the 1990s, and more timid regulators later allowed the automakers to take those cars off the streets and crush them, erasing the evidence that consumers once had the option to choose clean cars. While electric cars were available, however, there were waiting lists of buyers. The zeal with which their drivers resisted automakers' attempts to destroy the cars impressed California regulators such that they may increase pressure on automakers to create clean vehicles when they revise state rules in 2007. What California does is important to the rest of the United States. California is the only state allowed to set clean-air regulations that are tougher than US federal standards. Other states may choose to follow the federal or the California standards.

Chapter 2 explains the similarities and differences between hybrids, plug-in hybrids, and electric vehicles. It examines the various advantages to running on electricity in terms of efficiency, cost, pollution reduction, and more. Readers who want a detailed manual of the mechanics and electrical components of plug-in hybrids won't find it here, but the organizations described in this book can point you to appropriate sources.

The arrival of immensely popular hybrids such as the Toyota Prius, Honda Insight, and Ford Escape SUV introduced hundreds of thousands of consumers to cars that incorporate some electricity for power but still rely on gasoline. In the geopolitical realities of the post-9/11 world, that dependence ultimately is the fatal flaw of hybrids. Unlike cars that can't run without gasoline, plug-in hybrids can use gasoline or cleaner, cheaper, domestic electricity — or both.

Biofuels such as ethanol or biodiesel may offer a homegrown alternative to gasoline, but producing enough biofuel to power all the cars, trucks, and SUVs in America is impossible today and impractical in the future. If we replace gasoline with biofuels in plug-in hybrids, however, the amount of liquid fuel needed could be cut to a fraction, because it's a backup for the electric drive. That makes biofuels a more realistic replacement for gasoline on a large scale.

Talk to anyone seeking the best way to get US transportation off petroleum and they're likely to say, "There's no silver bullet." There's no single solution. I agree. Rather than searching for a single bullet to kill off gasoline, I like to think that the best minds are finding solutions that will work together to let us live well without gasoline.

Smarter urban planning, more use of public transit, bicycling, walking, car-sharing, and ride-sharing are important parts of solving the problems that automobiles have brought us. There's more than one rung in the ladder to get us off of petroleum. By focusing this book on just one rung — plug-in hybrids — I do not mean to slight any of these other important strategies.

Chapter 3 answers a common and important question related to plug-in hybrids: What about hydrogen? Aren't hydrogen fuel-cell vehicles supposed to be the clean, green cars of the future? I argue that hydrogen will never make sense for cars. Even if you think it does, nearly everyone agrees it will be decades before there will be hydrogen fuel-cell cars and more than a few fueling stations, if ever. If we don't do something much, much sooner to decrease global warming emissions from vehicles, we're toast. Reducing our need for imported oil is a priority that can't wait decades. Plug-in hybrids can meet both those goals with technology that's here today and that doesn't require any new, expensive infrastructure like expensive hydrogen fueling stations.

Chapter 4 describes the plug-in hybrids that have been made so far and looks at the technological readiness for mass production. Bringing them to market doesn't necessarily mean they'll stay available, however, as the battle to save electric vehicles from being crushed by automakers reminds us in chapter 5.

I explore the most common concern expressed about plug-in hybrids and electric vehicles in chapter 6: Are they really that clean? What about polluting, electrical power plants? The electricity has to come from somewhere. The same is true of gasoline; it doesn't just magically appear out of nowhere. I'll present evidence that plug-in cars reduce greenhouse gases and most other pollutants compared with either hybrids or conventional non-hybrid cars, even when accounting for pollution from power plants. Plus, plug-in hybrids let us take greater advantage of renewable power from wind and solar energy and move us closer to a sustainable society.

For all these reasons, plug-in hybrids have caught the fancy of folks from all parts of the political spectrum. Chapters 7 and 8 describe how and why conservatives' concerns for national security prompted them to become champions of plug-in hybrids. They hooked up with more progressive activists and middle-of-theroaders, and, as described in chapter 9, formed a diverse cast of characters backing plug-in hybrids.

We follow some of them in this book — an automotive insider, engineers and environmentalists, streetwise political activists, and a neoconservative former CIA director. Parts of the book are reconstructions of conversations and events based on interviews with the participants.

Many, many people are integral to the story of plug-in hybrids. The ones highlighted in this book are not necessarily the most prominent or the most important, but they played key roles that allow me to present plug-in hybrids in what I hope is an enjoyable fashion. These include:

- Chelsea Sexton, automotive insider. Working for General Motors, Sexton fought attempts to destroy the electric EV1 car. Her experience illustrates how car companies are resisting plug-in cars, and why they'll make them anyway.
- Felix Kramer and the tech squad. Geek power, in all the best meanings of the phrase, put plug-in hybrids on the public map. Hackers with expertise in computers and cars turned a Toyota Prius into a 100 miles-per-gallon (160 km-per-gallon) plug-in hybrid and brought it to the attention of the world. What they did, the car companies will do even better, and on a much larger scale.
- Marc Geller, grassroots activist. Inspired by the successful protests of Act Up, Queer Nation, and anti-war activists, Geller helped organize street demonstrations that shamed some car companies into ceasing destruction of electric vehicles. The actions put the lie to automakers' claims that nobody wants plug-in cars, and helped pave the way for plug-in hybrids.
- R. James Woolsey, former CIA director and national security hawk. Seeing the end of cheap oil supplies looming, Woolsey advocates for plug-in hybrids to wean us from petroleum and to divert former "petrodollars" away from Islamic radicals. Conservatives in high office are being influenced by his arguments.

I don't necessarily agree with all the views of the various

people described in this book, but I present them to explain why plug-in hybrids have generated such widespread support.

A convergence of forces — stretching from progressive environmental groups all the way to the ex-oilman in the White House — suggest that plug-in hybrids will soon be available, as described in chapter 10. And chapter 11 gives you some tools to help hasten their arrival.

If politics is the art of compromise, plug-in hybrids may be the most political cars of all time. The story of how their time has come is a cautionary tale, though. The oil and auto companies know how to undermine the success of plug-in car programs to protect the status quo. With the information and the tools presented in this book, readers can help ensure that plug-in hybrids not only get to market, but stay here.

Let's get to it.

THE AUTOMOTIVE INSIDERS

CHAPTER 1

Chelsea Sexton Finds a Home

S HE HADN'T MEANT TO CRY, but Chelsea Sexton couldn't help it. Giving a eulogy at a funeral for your first love can make it hard to keep your eyes dry. She pushed her straight red hair behind one ear and looked out at the crowd of 200 or so mourners seated under a canopy at the Hollywood Forever Cemetery.

All the usual funeral clichés fit the deceased. Died too soon. So much potential. Why, why, why? Sorely missed. Gone but not forgotten.

Sexton looked at her husband, Bob, who also had loved the deceased. In fact, if it hadn't been for Sexton's first love, she and Bob never would have met, eloped, and had a baby. But this funeral represented more than a single death, more than a sentimental loss of a family member. This was the death of a dream.

She took a deep breath and spoke: "I have come here today to mourn the loss of the EV1." Heads turned to look at the sleek, silver, rocket-shaped electric car, its windshield shrouded in black cloth, and a huge bouquet of flowers resting on its hood.

Born in the minds of General Motors (GM) Corporation engineers in collaboration with a group of avant-garde engineers in

Southern California called AeroVironment, the first EV1 (initially called the Impact) debuted in January, 1990, at the Los Angeles Auto Show. The EV1 had been hand-built in a hurry to make GM look good and was nowhere near ready for production. But Chairman Jack Smith introduced it, saying that "issues like global climate warming and energy conservation demand fundamental change from all industries in all nations." After the car made a splash at the auto show and in the media, GM quietly put a team together to see if the EV1 could and should become part of its lineup of cars and trucks.[1]

American consumers have come to expect that the futuristic prototypes that car companies display with such pizzazz at auto shows aren't real: Nothing they'll ever be able to buy, just dreams, really. They gawk and drool over these possibilities and then go back to buying the same old internal combustion engine cars that we've had for a century instead of demanding the innovations dangled before them.

One group of Californians in 1990 apparently didn't know that's the way the game is played. The EV1 caught the eye of the California Air Resources Board (CARB), a regulatory body searching for ways to meet the state's Clean Air Act and clear its smoggy skies. The EV1's power came from batteries that got recharged at night when the car was plugged in. It had no engine, no tailpipe, and no emissions. If GM was boasting that it could build a clean car, why not take them up on it? And why not expect the same of the other automakers?

In September of 1990, CARB declared that if auto companies wanted to do business in state, they would have to produce zero-emission vehicles to the tune of 2% of California sales by 1998, increasing to 5% by 2001, and 10% by 2003.

That Zero-Emission Vehicle (ZEV) Mandate might as well have been the kiss of death for the EV1. It's one thing for an automaker to think it has a one-of-a-kind model — the next hot thing. Tell the company that all of its competitors will have to make essentially the same thing, ensuring tough competition, and the car's shine starts to fade. The major automakers have a long history of resisting when told what to do, pouring millions of dollars into fighting government mandates that eventually get incorporated into cars anyway. Things like seat belts, air bags, catalytic converters, and better fuel efficiency all were fought by automakers.

Between 1922 and 1955, GM colluded with Standard Oil and the Firestone tire company to systematically buy up the nation's clean (electric) and popular streetcar systems, the dominant mode of public urban transportation.[2] By 1946, using a front company called National City Lines, they owned streetcar lines in 80 cities and steadily closed them down, replacing them with exhaust-belching, unpopular buses. At the same time, they lobbied hard for creation of interstate highways and the paving of America's cities with freeways in order to promote car use. A federal antitrust investigation led to conviction of GM executives, but by then US public electric transportation was obliterated, and the company paid only $5,000 in fines.

Time and again automakers have resisted making safety and environmental improvements to their vehicles.[3] A Ford representative insisted in 1953 that car exhaust was not related to air pollution, even though the Los Angeles Air Pollution Control District confirmed the connection. In 1971 Ford President Lee Iacocca complained to President Richard Nixon that shoulder belts and headrests were complete wastes of money. He felt the same way about air bags. A GM vice president, Earnest Starkman, testified before the US Congress in 1972 that mandates for catalytic converters on 1975 models could shutter the company. After the automakers installed them, they survived. Publicly, GM, Ford, and Chrysler have dismissed acid rain as a serious problem, fought fuel-economy standards (and then met them), attacked the 1970 Clean Air Act, claimed that electric vehicles couldn't be produced (and then made them), and fought against limits on greenhouse gas emissions (a struggle that's now in the courts).

With the electric cars, GM executives faced a particularly significant problem. Sincerely marketing an electric car on its merits — pointing out that it is quiet, efficient, easy to maintain, inexpensive on fuel, doesn't pollute, and reduces the nation's dependence on gasoline and oil — could sully the image of the company's core products. What does that say about larger and more complex cars, trucks, and sport utility vehicles (SUVs) that use gasoline and spew nasty fumes out their tailpipes?

Factions within GM believed the EV1 to be progress on a revolutionary scale. Other factions felt that it would never catch on with the public and was dead in the water. The initial investment that would be required, a given for any new technology, staggered some GM executives as the company struggled to find its financial footing in the 1990s. Others in the company saw the EV1 as a way for GM to capture top position in making the cars of the future.

Whether or not GM's executives really wanted the EV1 to succeed — and they say that they did — was a moot point. Other than electric vehicles, there was no other kind of ZEV in sight. Build it they must. The same went for the other automakers. The reluctant race to build plug-in cars was on.

THE FIRST MODERN ELECTRIC CAR DEBUTS

In 1996, to market this totally new brand of car and find consumers to lease the EV1s, GM hired a team of 13 very young, mostly white, clean-cut, and relatively inexperienced employees, including Chelsea. They were all made to read *The Car That Could: The Inside Story of GM's Revolutionary Electric Vehicle*.[4] The 1996 book by *Vanity Fair* contributor Michael Schnayerson described how the EV1 nearly died stillborn due to internal company conflicts and budget cuts, but lived to see the light of day.

When the first EV1s to be offered to the public were ready in December of 1996, "We had a huge sense of the world on our shoulders," Sexton said. GM gave the EV1 Specialists, as they were called, some training and then essentially wished them luck and cut them loose. The team operated as a lean, nimble unit, off the radar of the usual corporate systems and tethers. Years later, Chelsea would look back at the Specialists as a sign of GM's conflicted support for the EV1: "When have they ever launched an entire new car brand with 13 people who've never done it before?"

For the Specialists, their work quickly became more than a job. It was a mission: To convince an interested but skeptical pub-

Sherry Boschert

Chelsea Sexton.

lic that plugging in a car was cleaner, cheaper, and more convenient than using gasoline.

The idea of plugging in a car seemed inconvenient because it was unfamiliar. Here's what powering the EV1 required: Pulling into your garage, getting out of the car, and plugging it in with a paddle-shaped charger, going about your home life, going to sleep, and waking up with a recharged car ready in the morning. Here's what refueling a gasoline car required: Driving away from home, finding a gasoline station, waiting in line, pulling up to the pump, getting out of the car, attaching the gasoline nozzle to the car, waiting, breathing noxious fumes, washing your hands, paying more for gasoline than you would for electricity, getting back in the car, driving home.

In this electronic age, with so many of the tools of modern life attached to power cords, the Specialists could use lots of examples to make customers more at ease with the idea of plugging in. People have become used to plugging in cellphones, personal digital assistants, camera battery rechargers, and hair curlers — why not cars?

If GM officials thought that they could wait a bit for the EV1 program to fail and then go back to the Air Resources Board and say that electric vehicles were a dud, they hadn't counted on the Specialists actually being able to do what they were hired to do. The Specialists took promotion of the EV1 to heart.

For Chelsea, her relationship with the EV1 became even bigger than that. Growing up as a smart but painfully shy girl, she had been "sort of an academic geek." She learned not to be intimidated by science or by being a girl in a guy's world. When she first landed a job in one of GM's Saturn showrooms in Los Angeles at the tender age of 17, she got really, really into cars — "on the far end of the spectrum in terms of geekiness," she says. What started as a job to help pay for college became more interesting than what she was studying. Chelsea stayed with Saturn for years.

She began dismantling broken parts, to see what was in them. She often visited with the company's engineers, to ask questions. When Chelsea walked in, the engineers hardly saw a geek. They were more than happy to share their knowledge. It wasn't every day that they had the rapt attention of a pretty 21-year-old.

So when the EV1 — the first modern electric car — came along, she could tell it was something special. The technology was new and sexy. Although the state demanded clean cars for environmental reasons, people leased the EV1s because they were cool and fast, the hot new thing. The engineering of the car took a back seat to sex appeal.

Second in line for the cars, though, were engineers who were intrigued by the electrical propulsion and battery components. It didn't hurt, of course, that even the frumpiest engineer suddenly attracted a lot of attention from women when driving an EV1. "Some who fought the hardest to keep their EV1s" when the car was being killed by off by GM were the engineers, she said.

Chelsea fell in love with the EV1. "At the age of 21, I had no way of knowing that a car would become my life," she recalled. But it wasn't her entire life. She noticed Bob Sexton, one of the EV1 service technicians. Bob had transferred to Chelsea's dealership from a previous Saturn outlet where the manager threw every obstacle he could think of into the EV1's path. Customers couldn't test drive them. Service technicians were not allowed to work on them. Bob really wanted to be an EV1 technician, so he asked to be transferred. At Chelsea's dealership he became one of two sought-after technicians known for their superb knowledge of the car and dedication to its success.

Chelsea and Bob dated by working on cars together. A romantic night for two was putting on jeans and pulling out the tools. Bob asked his boss for permission to work on EV1 marketing events with Chelsea. "ChelseaandBob" became one word around the company. The two eloped, and had a son, Christopher. The baby sometimes slept above his dad in an EV1 while Bob worked on the car from below.

"If I do my job well," thought Chelsea, "my son will never need to know a world without electric vehicles."

She couldn't have dreamed that a few years later this definition of her job would find her camped outside a parking lot in a public vigil, trying to save the last 78 remaining EV1s, with her son writing in chalk on the sidewalk: "I love the EV1, don't crush the EV1, love Chris age 6."

CORPORATE CONFLICTS

GM and the other automakers worked to meet California's ZEV Mandate and fought it at the same time. By the time the Specialists handed the keys to the first lucky EV1 customer, state regulators already had backed off from the 1998 and 2001 ZEV requirements. Instead, the seven major car companies each signed an individual Memorandum of Agreement with CARB to produce a small number of electric vehicles by 2000 as a demonstration of their viability, and to make ZEVs 10% of sales in 2003.

GM initially built 660 EV1s using lead-acid battery packs, many of which were defective and didn't come close to meeting the 70- to 90-mile range per charge provided by good batteries. The car wasn't perfect; some of the early ones leaked water into the electronics when it rained, swayed under acceleration, and had design flaws in the charging mechanism, all problems that were fixed in the second-generation model and didn't appear in some competitors' electric vehicles. Leases were expensive, and few public charging stations had been installed.

Despite these and other problems with the "Generation I" EV1s, Chelsea and the other Specialists managed to lease every one of the cars. "The Specialists knew we were now responsible for the dreams of the hundreds of people who had designed, built, and fought in various ways for that car to happen," she said.

In 1999 GM released the last 182 EV1s required of it by 2000, this time with a better, nickel-metal-hydride (NiMH) battery pack that allowed the car to go 140 miles (224 km) before needing recharging. Although range has always been the weak spot of electric vehicles, plenty of people considered this sufficient for daily driving, and plenty of them wanted the new EV1.

News of the car's better batteries, design improvements, and popularity may not have trickled up to corporate bean-counters. From their point of view, it was an expensive car with problems, and GM was in a financial slump, looking to cut costs. One month before abandoning the EV1, GM bought the Hummer brand and started to ramp up its marketing of the most wasteful car in history.

Although GM's Memorandum of Agreement with CARB required the company to produce some EV1s in 2000 as well, in 1999 GM shut down the car's assembly line, this time permanently.

The state government offered subsidies to bring the lease down to a reasonable level, in some cases as low as $250 per month, to assist the infant EV industry. More public charging stations were installed across the state. With orders still coming in and no cars to provide, the Specialists started a waiting list that eventually grew to 5,000 names. They begged GM to restart production and send them more cars. The company said that it would if there was enough demand. Sexton never could get anyone to define "enough demand" with a number.

GM designed other versions of the EV1 but never marketed them. The company hired Andrew Frank, professor at the University of California, Davis, to make a plug-in hybrid version of the EV1 in the mid-1990s — one that had both a gasoline engine and batteries that could be plugged in for recharging. A conventional hybrid version was created too. The public saw them only as concept cars on display at GM events.

GM's EV1 was the only car offered to the public that was built from the ground up as an electric vehicle by a major company. (Honda claimed its EV Plus was, too, but others say the company converted a gasoline model that had been sold in Japan.) Besides GM, other automakers met the ZEV Mandate by converting existing vehicles into electrics. The vehicles worked, but not as elegantly as cars optimized to run on electricity. To CARB, some of the companies showed their own prototypes of aerodynamic, from-the-ground-up electric vehicles, but that's not what they showed to customers. What they gave the public was "crap" compared with what they could have produced, one insider said. Most leaseholders still loved what they got; they just didn't know they could have gotten better.

To comply with the ZEV Mandate, Chevrolet (part of GM) added batteries to some S-10 pickup trucks. Chrysler leased 50 Electric Powered Interurban Commuter (EPIC) minivans to utilities in the early 1990s. In 1997 it introduced the electric TEVan and eventually leased about 2,000 of them to government and utility fleets in California and New York. Ford introduced an electric Ecostar van in 1993 and switched emphasis to electric Ranger pickups in 1997, eventually leasing about 200 of them to individuals and 1,500 to commercial fleets. Ford also bought a Norwegian company in order to lease 440 of its electric Th!nk-City cars.

While all this was happening, the car companies and the oil companies poured millions of dollars into both overt and covert campaigns to get CARB to drop the ZEV Mandate. GM later would claim (and still claims today) that it spent $1 billion to develop, market, and support the EV1, but an article in *Automotive News* in 1998 put the figure at $350 million for EV1 development. People outside the company estimate that GM may have spent up to $600 million on its multi-year lobbying and public relations campaigns to kill the ZEV Mandate, so perhaps the $1 billion figure is the total spent to create and to kill the EV1.

Because nine other US states were threatening to adopt emissions standards similar to California's, the car and oil companies fought tooth and nail to get rid of the California Mandate. The American Automobile Manufacturers Association spent $500,000 on public relations firm Cerrell Associates in a mere six months of 1995 to turn public sentiment against the ZEV Mandate. The Western States Petroleum Association, one of the top employers of California lobbyists, hired another PR firm to coordinate an extensive anti-ZEV Mandate campaign along with its front group, Californians Against Hidden Taxes. They ran media ads, complained on conservative talk radio, delayed the regulatory process with multiple requests for data, and bussed seniors to hearings to protest a proposed six-cents-per-month surcharge on utility bills to support electric charging stations.

Compared with other car models, electric vehicles got little advertising, and what did exist often was incomplete, confusing, or negative. No commercials with sexy models in electric cars powering past competitors. No ads with satisfied "customers" explaining how well the cars suited them. No details on how or where to get an electric car.

One GM ad for the EV1 put it this way: "'How does it go without gas and air? How does it go without sparks and explosions? How does it go without need for transmission? How does it go?' you ask yourself. And then you will ask, 'How did we go so long without it?' The electric car. It isn't coming. It's here."

When people did ask about leasing an electric car, many car dealers claimed ignorance or said the cars were not available or were slow to respond. They usually tried to steer customers away from the electric car and toward a gasoline model. The tactics worked. Although an industry-sponsored poll initially showed that the public was interested in buying electric vehicles, some later polls reflected a more doubtful and skeptical public.

After getting the ZEV Mandate for 1998 and 2001 lifted, the major automakers still faced the requirement of 10% clean cars by 2003. Repeatedly, they made their case to CARB: These cars would never be affordable, they didn't work well enough, and besides, nobody wanted them.

In February of 2001, at a weekly meeting in Detroit of the EV1 brand team and GM lawyers who were preparing the lawsuit, the lawyers made it clear that waiting lists for EV1s were unacceptable. How could they argue that no one wanted these cars if there was a waiting list? "If it weren't for the goddamn EV1 Specialists, we wouldn't have this problem," one said.[5] The word came down to the Specialists team within minutes, in another conference call: The waiting lists didn't exist. No one could speak of it.

By then the Specialists had kept the EV1 program going years longer than most people in GM had expected. The team could read the writing on the wall, though. With the ZEV Mandate being eviscerated and the automakers planning to sue, there was little hope that GM would actually restart production of the EV1. Most of the Specialists left for other jobs. Not Chelsea. She stayed on as long as she could, trying to get the last EV1s into the hands of people eager to lease them.

In late 2001, GM and Chrysler sued California to block the ZEV Mandate. GM also laid off Chelsea Sexton and the last of the EV1 Specialists. Grateful EV1 drivers baked a cake and threw a party for Chelsea and the other two Specialists who were now out of a job.

In the end, although the company made a total of 1,135 EV1s, only about 800 of them were available to the public for leasing. For years GM executives stated that the company only managed to lease around 800 of the cars, citing that as evidence that there was no market for electric vehicles, without acknowledging that they had leased all the ones they had made available. The Specialists couldn't refute the company line in public because of nondisclosure agreements they'd been made to sign when hired. It wasn't until 2005 that a GM executive admitted to the media that there had, indeed, been a waiting list for the EV1, freeing Chelsea to talk about it openly. By then the company had rounded up all but 78 or so of the EV1s, hauled them off to Arizona, and crushed them flat.

The day of the EV1 funeral, though, the black-clad mourners in Hollywood didn't want to picture such a final, gruesome ending to what they considered one of the greatest cars ever made.

The ZEV Mandate had withered away, but at least the electric vehicles that had been made were still on the road, proof that it was possible.

CARB had watered down the ZEV Mandate not only in 1996 but in 1998, in 2001, and again several months before the 2003 funeral for the EV1. The 2003 changes gave automakers the option of meeting requirements by making a handful of hydrogen fuel-cell vehicles for demonstration purposes, even if they weren't in California, and larger numbers of gasoline-dependent hybrid vehicles or plug-in hybrids. Electric vehicles still could meet the Mandate, but now there also was a way to comply without building them.[6]

Four months before that fateful decision, Alan Lloyd, PhD, the chairman of the Air Resources Board, also had become chairman of the California Fuel Cell Partnership. He flatly rejected complaints of a conflict of interest.[7] Theoretical hydrogen fuel-cell cars had emerged as the only possible zero-emission cars that might compete with electric vehicles. The car companies were dangling their willing participation in hydrogen fuel-cell programs to show that they were doing something to create cleaner cars. After the lawsuit that the automakers had filed against the Mandate in 2002, the possibility of cooperation from the car companies was enticing to state regulators.

CARB went along with the hydrogen scenario, even though this technology would not be usable for decades, if ever. Board members expanded on a set of oxymoronic categories like "partial zero-emissions vehicles" that permitted gasoline cars to fulfill clean-air requirements. No longer did anyone actually have to produce ZEVs in meaningful quantities, at least not soon. Although the 2003 regulations would go into effect in 2005, auto companies had banked enough credits by placing over 4,000 electric vehicles on the road between 1998 and 2003 that they didn't need to do more for years.

In 2001 CARB had created a new category, "alternative technology partial zero-emission vehicles" (AT-PZEVs), to give extra credit to hybrids and especially plug-in hybrids with a 20-mile (32-km) all-electric range. To further promote production of plug-in hybrids, CARB redefined them in 2003 as vehicles that could run at least 10 miles (16 km) on electricity before using gasoline and made them worth more than 10 times as many credits as hybrids, though still less than electric or hydrogen vehicles.

Critics saw the 2003 decisions as eviscerating the ZEV Mandate, but CARB considered them to be building blocks for eventual reintroduction of clean cars. Hybrids, plug-in hybrids, and fuel-cell vehicles share many of the same components as electric vehicles. Making them would help bring down costs for the electric components and let both automakers and consumers get more comfortable with the idea of a car being partly electric.

"We believe that they are accelerating our progress toward our ultimate goal, which is zero-emission vehicles. We're particularly happy with how this AT-PZEV portion of our regulation has worked out," CARB's Craig Childers told members of the Electric Drive Transportation Association at a December 2005 meeting.

Still, the 2003 modifications created loopholes the size of a semi-trailer for companies that didn't want to make ZEVs, at least through 2008. CARB had a real possibility for zero-emission electric vehicles in its grasp, but let it go by repeatedly weakening the original ZEV Mandate. Jananne Sharpless, a former CARB chair, said later: "They gave it away. To me, that's just sad. It's a sad commentary on the way our society and our system in the United States works."[8]

After the 2003 changes to the ZEV Mandate made electric vehicles unnecessary, GM and the other automakers officially canceled their electric-car programs, which they'd already mothballed. Fans of the EV1 still had some hope that GM might continue to lease the existing cars, however, or maybe even sell them to the leaseholders.

GOODBYE, FOR NOW

On that warm July 24, 2003, in Hollywood Forever Cemetery, a solemn bagpiper led the funeral procession of sleek EV1s. The mourners had gathered at the invitation of Sexton and Chris Paine, a filmmaker and former EV1 driver (with a license plate reading EV RIDR). They summoned current and former lease-holders, EV1 engineers, and drivers of the other endangered electric cars to the ceremony, which would be part of a documentary on the promise and the demise of the electric vehicle.[9]

In the cemetery of Hollywood stars, actor and conservationist Ed Begley, Jr. lionized the EV1. "It's true that electric cars will not meet the needs of all Americans," he said. "They'll only meet the needs of 90% of Americans."

Baywatch actress Alexandra Paul paid her respects. EV1 engineer Wally Rippel of AeroVironment described his admiration for the car. Sexton's son Christopher, then age four, didn't really understand what was happening to "mama's cool electric car" but could tell that something was wrong. Others who had driven electric cars were there in spirit if not in person — Tom Hanks, Jay Leno, Mel Gibson, Robin Williams, Danny DeVito, Julia Louis Dreyfus, Tony Shalhoub, and others.

The sun glinted off Sexton's silver earring, and her eyes glistened when she thanked everyone there for their passion and dedication in furthering the dream of a better, cleaner car. "This is a dream that does not die easily," she said, rededicating herself to accomplish the mission for which GM had hired her.

We never know where pursuit of dreams will take us. If someone at the EV1 funeral had told Sexton that within two years she would be strategizing with a former CIA director, trying to forge an alliance in support of new plug-in cars, she would have laughed.

But knowing the technology as she did, and how much sense it makes, nothing could shake her confidence in the inevitability of cars that plug in, whether all-electric vehicles or plug-in hybrids. "Whether a big automaker does it or not, someone will step up to the plate to mass-produce" electric vehicles or plug-in hybrids, says Sexton, "and that person will change the world."

Zero-Emission Vehicle (ZEV) Mandate Timeline[10]

▌1990
- General Motors (GM) displays Impact (later called EV1) electric car.
- California Air Resources Board (CARB) then requires top seven automakers (GM, Ford, Chrysler, Honda, Toyota, Nissan, and Mazda) to make 2% of sales in the state be zero-emission vehicles (ZEVs) by 1998, 5% by 2001, and 10% by 2003. Smaller carmakers like Volkswagen, BMW, and Mitsubishi would have to start offering ZEVs in 2003.

▌1991
- Nine northeastern states adopt parts of California's regulations.

▌1992
- Volvo displays Environmental Concept Car (ECC), a plug-in hybrid.

▌1993
- Chrysler is first to deliver commercialized EVs — five TEVans — to New York utilities.
- The Big 3 (GM, Ford, and Chrysler) sue New York and Massachusetts to fight ZEV Mandates.
- California utilities ask for six-cents-a-month surcharge on ratepayers to fund infrastructure and incentives for ZEVs. Western States Petroleum Association hires public relations firm to create a "grassroots" campaign to block the surcharge and attack the ZEV Mandate.

▌1994
- Energy Conversion Devices (ECD) puts nickel-metal-hydride (NiMH) batteries in an EV1 body; it goes 201 miles (322 km) at 55 miles (88 km) per hour, or 135 miles (216 km) in city driving, and sets electric land speed record at 183 miles (293 km) per hour. NiMH in a Solectria four-seater sedan has a 174-mile range (278 km).
- GM enters joint partnership with ECD, with 60% share to GM.

- Head of US Advanced Battery Consortium (made up of the Big 3 and US Department of Energy) testifies to CARB that NiMH battery isn't good enough yet.
- New York and Massachusetts win court ruling allowing ZEV Mandate.
- ECD wins lawsuit against Japanese companies for copying NiMH, and they become licensees.

1995
- The Big 3 boost funding for the American Automobile Manufacturers Association (AAMA) lobbying from $20 million to $34 million/year and spend $500,000 in six months on PR campaign against ZEV Mandate.
- Western States Petroleum Association funds $1 million PR campaign, blitzing California news media to raise doubts about electric vehicles.
- CARB holds technical review of battery technology; GM convinces them commercial NiMH batteries won't be ready until 2000.

1996
- NiMH in a Solectria sedan goes 375 miles (600 km) on a single charge.
- CARB accepts the major carmakers' proposals (known as Memoranda of Agreement) to make more than 1,800 ZEVs (instead of 60,000) by 2000 and to make all US gasoline cars by 2001 meet new federal low-emission standards; in exchange, CARB drops 1998 and 2001 ZEV targets. Companies are allowed to trade and bank credits to meet the 2003 goal of 10% ZEVs, with one credit for each ZEV made "available."
- Mitsubishi builds demonstration plug-in hybrid for CARB; Volvo and Nissan lobby CARB unsuccessfully for credits for plug-in hybrids.
- GM begins leasing the EV1.

1997
- After making 660 EV1s, GM shuts down assembly line.
- Other carmakers start leasing small numbers of electric vehicles.

1998

- CARB allows cars with emissions to meet ZEV Mandate. Although 4% of sales in 2003 must be ZEVs, 60% of that can be "partial zero-emission vehicles" or PZEVs (with fewer tailpipe emissions, zero evaporative emissions, other improvements) and "super ultra low emission vehicles" or SULEVs (relatively clean gasoline vehicles or natural-gas vehicles).
- Mercedes-Benz plans sales of A-Class electric vehicle but program is shut down when parent company Daimler-Benz merges with Chrysler.
- ECD converts a Toyota Prius to a demonstration plug-in hybrid; it goes 20 miles (32 km) on electricity alone and gets 70–80 miles (112–128 km) per gallon of gasoline.

1999

- GM releases 182 more EV1s (this time with NiMH batteries) to meet CARB's 2000 deadline, then ends production permanently.
- Volvo begins making a plug-in hybrid but is bought by Ford, which shuts the program down.
- CARB is forced to accept neighborhood electric vehicles (NEVs, top speed 25 miles [40 km] per hour) for ZEV credit by ruling of US Department of Transportation.

2000

- CARB analysis finds ZEV Mandate is economically viable. Volume production of 100,000 ZEVs per year would make lifecycle costs competitive with conventional vehicles.
- Texaco buys GM's share of partnership with ECD and creates 50/50 ownership with ECD in spinoff battery company, Cobasys (which controls NiMH patent).

2001

- CARB cuts ZEV Mandate for 2003 to 2% of sales plus 2% "advance technology PZEVs" (AT-PZEVs, mainly hybrids or plug-in hybrids with 20-mile electric range) and 6% PZEVs. Target would gradually increase to 10% ZEVs by 2018. CARB also reduces credit for NEVs and adds complexities including partial credit for "vehicle efficiency."

- GM, Daimler Chrysler, and a few dealers file lawsuit claiming that the ZEV Mandate's clauses on efficiency usurp federal control over fuel economy standards.
- University of California, Davis, holds workshop on "Meeting the New CARB ZEV Mandate Requirements: Grid-Connected Hybrids and City EVs."
- President George W. Bush announces $1.2 billion Hydrogen Fuel Initiative.

2002

- Court injunction prohibits enforcement of ZEV Mandate during litigation.
- GM declares EV1 leases will not be renewed. Ford cancels electric Th!nkCity car program.
- Toyota sells electric RAV4-EV for a few months, then stops taking orders for sales or leases.
- Most car companies have banked enough ZEV credits to last through 2006 or later.
- Federal lawyers under Bush administration back the automakers in lawsuit against California.
- Federal tax credit for EVs: Up to $4,000. Federal tax credit for largest SUVs: Up to $100,000.
- Federal court blocks ZEV Mandate. CARB considers reverting to 1999 version.
- Court issues preliminary injunction against 1999 ZEV regulations.
- California adopts Pavley Clean Car Bill (AB1493) to reduce greenhouse gas emissions from vehicles by 30% from 2009 to 2016.
- Southern California Edison tests provide strong evidence that NiMH batteries in Toyota RAV4-EVs will last 130,000–150,000 miles (208,000–240,000 km). The utility's fleet of 320 RAV4-EVs drove nearly 7 million miles (11.2 million km) in five years with no gasoline or oil, eliminating 830 tons (753 metric tons) of air pollutants and preventing more than 3,700 tons (3,357 metric tons) of tailpipe carbon dioxide emissions.
- CARB Chairman Alan Lloyd also named chair of California Fuel Cell Partnership.

▌ **2003**
- CARB deletes any mention of efficiency or fuel economy from ZEV Mandate. Gives automakers the option of building 250 fuel-cell vehicles each in any state by 2008 and meeting rest of ZEV Mandate by selling hybrids or plug-in hybrids with 10-mile electric range. Numbers of vehicles to increase over time.
- Automakers formally cancel all electric-vehicle programs and end litigation.
- Environmental Protection Agency under Bush administration says it has no authority to regulate greenhouse gas emissions from vehicles.

▌ **2004**
- As electric-vehicle leases end, automakers repossess and destroy the cars.
- Protests at Ford facilities in US and Norway convince Ford to spare remaining electric Th!nkCity cars.
- California Governor Arnold Schwarzenegger announces "Hydrogen Highway" to spend millions on fueling stations for fuel-cell vehicles.
- Alliance of Automobile Manufacturers (AAM, formerly the AAMA) sues to block California greenhouse gas regulations.

▌ **2005**
- Nine states adopt California's vehicle greenhouse gas emissions limits (Connecticut, Maine, Massachusetts, New Jersey, New York, Oregon, Rhode Island, Vermont, and Washington).
- Automakers agree to California-like emissions limits in Canada: reduce greenhouse gases by 25%, or 5.3 million tons (4.8 million metric tons), by end of 2010.
- Vigil outside Ford dealer persuades company to sell remaining electric Ranger trucks rather than destroy them.
- Protests at Toyota events and facilities convince company to extend remaining leases on electric RAV4-EV SUVs rather than destroy them.
- Protests fail to sway GM, which destroys the EV1s.
- California's Hydrogen Highway program gets $6.5 million for three fueling stations and leases of small number of vehicles.

▌ 2006

- US Supreme Court agrees to hear suit by 12 states to determine whether Environmental Protection Agency should regulate vehicle greenhouse gas emissions.
- Toyota officials say next-generation Prius will be a plug-in hybrid.
- Saab (a GM subsidiary) displays a convertible plug-in hybrid that runs on 100% ethanol and electricity at Swedish auto show, but GM rewrites press release to delete reference to plug.
- CARB holds ZEV Mandate technical review.

▌ 2007

- Automakers' suit against California's greenhouse gas emissions law scheduled for trial.
- Probable modification of ZEV regulations.

CHAPTER 2

Will the Circuit be Unbroken?

IN THE 1990S, the GM EV1 had one official spokesperson — Bill Nye the Science Guy, host of the popular Public Broadcasting System program of the same name. By 2006 Nye instead was the celebrity host of the Union of Concerned Scientists' website HybridCenter.org, where he not-so-scientifically promoted hybrids. On a page entitled, "Plugging in is a myth," Nye proclaimed that with his gasoline-powered hybrid, "I get the high performance, low emissions, and great mileage without getting electric energy from anywhere but the car's own built-in electrical system." Somehow the Science Guy missed the fact that the hybrid's batteries get their charge mainly from the car's greenhouse-gas producing, mobile generator — the internal combustion engine.

How did it come to this?

HYBRIDS, PLUG-IN HYBRIDS, AND ELECTRIC VEHICLES

Once the major car companies were freed from making zero-emission vehicles (ZEVs) in any significant quantity, electric vehicles were forgotten by the mainstream, but not entirely gone.

Credit: Electric Drive Transportation Association (EDTA).

Compared with conventional hybrid-electric vehicles (HEVs), the drivetrains of plug-in hybrid-electric vehicles (PHEVs) or pure battery-electric vehicles (BEVs) use more batteries, a larger electric motor, and a smaller (or no) gasoline combustion engine.

In fact, what soon became the greenest car with the longest waiting list of buyers, the car that generated the greatest buzz — the hybrid gasoline-electric vehicle — pegged its success on components borrowed from electric vehicles. So much so that many hybrid drivers mistakenly think that they drive electric cars.

What's the difference? Let's start with some definitions.

Electric vehicles: These are cars, trucks, and sport utility vehicles (SUVs) powered by an electric motor, one or more controllers, and a large bank of batteries. No gasoline engine. Electric vehicles plug into a wall socket or other source of electricity to recharge the batteries. When the driver steps on the accelerator pedal, the controller governs the amount of electricity that flows from the batteries to the motor that changes the electrical energy to mechanical energy, making the vehicle move.

Regenerative braking systems use the electric motor to convert some of the car's kinetic energy (the energy associated with a car in motion) into electricity that gets fed back into the batteries when the driver wants to slow down or stop. In conventional cars, that kinetic energy simply becomes heat on the mechanical brakes used to stop the car and is wasted.

Although homemade conversions of gasoline vehicles to electric vehicles usually plug into regular wall sockets, electric vehicles made by major auto companies came with special chargers that plugged into 220-volt sockets (the kind used for clothes dryers) to provide a faster charge.

Hybrids: Gasoline vehicles with internal combustion engines, hybrids also have an electric motor and a small bank of batteries that assist the engine, providing boosts of power or extending the range the vehicle can go. Hybrids can't be plugged in but use the gasoline engine motor plus regenerative braking to recharge the battery. In a hybrid, the gasoline engine shuts down when the vehicle is idle, saving energy and reducing emissions, and restarts seamlessly when the driver steps on the accelerator.

Hybrids come in three basic flavors: series hybrids, parallel hybrids, or combination series-parallel hybrids. A hybrid with a series drivetrain uses only the electric motor to turn the car's wheels using power from either the batteries or from a generator. The gasoline engine runs the generator and recharges the batteries, which also take advantage of regenerative braking. Series hybrids are most efficient in stop-and-go driving. For the most part, automakers have bypassed series hybrids in favor of parallel or series-parallel hybrids for passenger cars.

A hybrid with a parallel drivetrain turns the wheels using both the engine and the electric motor, working together with the help of computer controls and a transmission. Parallel hybrids are most efficient in highway driving. The first hybrid sold in the United States was a parallel hybrid — the Honda Insight. Most parallel hybrids do not allow electric-only propulsion.

The series-parallel hybrid drivetrain, popularized in the Toyota Prius, combines the two designs, allowing the gasoline engine to drive the wheels or be disconnected temporarily so that only the electric motor drives the wheels.

The fuel efficiency of hybrids depends on whether they are "full" hybrids that include all the hybrid features or "hollow" hybrids that claim the name but incorporate only one or two features, such as stopping the engine while idling but not incorporating regenerative braking. Full hybrid sedans can get 40–50 miles (64–80 km) per gallon. Hollow hybrids may improve gas mileage by a meager 1 mile per gallon.

Plug-in hybrids: Hybrids can be improved by adding more batteries, a charger, and an electrical plug. The first plug-in hybrids take advantage of Toyota's series-parallel drivetrain and add a few more batteries and a way to plug in for recharging, thus allowing longer driving in electric mode, using less gasoline, and producing fewer emissions. By plugging into a regular wall socket overnight while the owner is sleeping, a plug-in Prius can get over 100 miles (160 km) per gallon of gasoline plus a small amount of cheap electricity. No special chargers or electrical sockets are needed, and drivers don't need to think about finding someplace to charge if they want to drive a long distance. If owners don't plug in overnight, a plug-in Prius operates like the normal hybrid, getting 40–50 miles (64–80 km) per gallon.

WHY HYBRIDS?

During the struggle over the ZEV Mandate in the 1990s, Detroit automakers made a feint toward producing hybrid cars as part of a "Dream Car" partnership with the federal government arranged by the Clinton–Gore administration. The goal: To build a hybrid that gets 80 miles per gallon (128 km) by 2004. In exchange, the administration would drop pursuit of regulations for higher fuel efficiency standards, which the automakers had fought off successfully for decades.

Renamed the Partnership for a New Generation of Vehicles, the industry–government program spent about $1.25 billion of taxpayers' money between 1993 and 2002 (and perhaps as much of the automakers' money) before morphing into FreedomCar to focus on hydrogen fuel-cell vehicles.[1] No US automakers commercialized a hybrid during those years, but Japanese automakers did. Excluded from the US-industry Partnership and fearful that Detroit would beat them to market with a new kind of car, the Japanese automakers commercialized their own hybrids. In 1997 Toyota introduced the first hybrid in Japan — the Prius.

In response GM unveiled a parallel hybrid version of the EV1 at an auto show in 1998. The four-seater, all-wheel-drive car supposedly could go from 0 to 60 miles (96 km) per hour in 7 seconds with a range of 550 miles (880 km) and a fuel economy of 80 miles

(128 km) per gallon.[2] GM said it would be ready for production in 2001. Alongside it, GM showed a prototype series hybrid — which ran for the first 40 miles (64 km) or so on electricity and then on a gasoline turbine engine — that purportedly went from 0 to 60 in 9 seconds, had a 350-mile range, and got 60 miles (96 km) per gallon. Neither car ever made it to a dealer showroom.

Much as the US automakers never really thought that electric vehicles would catch on, they didn't think much of hybrids either. They publicly abandoned hybrids and left them to the Japanese automakers, who rode them to popularity and profits, changing the auto industry as they went.

When gasoline prices spiked in 2005, the auto industry rushed to produce more hybrids to meet consumer demand for more-efficient cars. The Toyota Prius, initially regarded as a niche car for affluent environmentalists, became a mainstream darling. Waiting lists kept buyers on hold for four to six months. Toyota planned to sell 300,000 Prius hybrids in 2006 and to sell 1 million hybrids a year by 2010, comprising more than 10% of its total sales. The market outpaced projections. By March 2006 Toyota sold more than half a million Prius hybrids and made plans to introduce many more hybrid models.

Ford developed its own hybrid technology, but it was so similar to Toyota's that it chose to license from its competitor rather than face patent struggles. Ford introduced the hybrid Escape compact SUV in 2005. Honda developed its own hybrid technology, was the first hybrid seller in North America, and is second in annual sales after Toyota. Other automakers have formed alliances to develop and sell their own hybrid systems — GM with DaimlerChrysler AG and BMW AG, and Volkswagon AG with Porsche AG.[3]

After the battle over the ZEV Mandate, consumers lost the electric cars and ended up with hybrids as the next best option. But enough drivers were exposed to electric vehicles that their advantages — the power of the plug — became more widely known. Some hybrid drivers began looking for ways to convert hybrids to plug-in hybrids. The popularity of hybrids introduced thousands more people who had missed the electric-vehicle era

to the benefits of having electricity in cars. The inevitable introduction of professionally manufactured plug-in hybrids will further that education and ultimately lead the market full circuit
back to production of electric vehicles.

The car companies don't necessarily want to make plug-in
hybrids, but they'll make them anyway. Why? To understand that,
it helps to know the strengths and weaknesses of electric vehicles.

IT'S ULTIMATELY ABOUT THE PLUG

The best thing and the worst thing about electric cars have always
been the same: You get to plug them in. You have to plug them in.
On the up side, plugging in means you don't need a smelly, noisy,
polluting gasoline engine. Drivers have the convenience of refueling at home. The fuel, electricity, is cheaper than gasoline and
domestically produced, meaning there's no need to rely on petroleum imports. The cars have no tailpipe and no emissions. If the
electricity comes from solar panels, windmills, or other renewable
sources, there's no pollution involved at all. You can make electricity for a car using solar panels on your home, but you can't
make even a drop of gasoline at home.

On the down side, when the car's batteries run out of juice,
you've got to plug in the car to recharge the batteries. Until recently, electric cars could go maybe 120–140 miles (192–224 km)
on a single charge, about half as far as the 300 or so miles (480
km) on a typical gasoline tank. With modern batteries, that gap
has narrowed, but state-of-the-art batteries are expensive. An
electric car's range depends mainly on the kind of batteries, the
number of batteries on board, the weight and shape of the car,
and how you drive it. A gasoline car's range depends mainly on
the size of the gasoline tank, the weight and shape of the car, and
how you drive it.

Let's look at some electric-car characteristics in a bit more
detail.

Noise: You don't need a muffler for an electric car because
there's nothing to muffle. There's no engine, no ignition. Turn the
key, and you might hear a few beeps or a slight hum. Press on the
pedal, and the car moves nearly silently. Imagine walking down a

street or riding a bicycle and not hearing engine noises from all the cars passing by. Cities would be quieter. Sound good?

Some people like noisy cars and trucks, though, because we've become used to equating noise with power. Would the Indianapolis 500 or monster-truck rallies be as thrilling without the deafening roar of engines? Just for laughs, a few electric-car drivers in California carry a CD in their cars that can play the sound of a revving engine in case they need it to mock, I mean, impress someone.

Because pedestrians and bicyclists expect to be able to hear gasoline cars that are backing out of driveways or passing them on the street, the switch to plug-in hybrids and electric cars will require a heightened alertness, at least until the number of gasoline cars decrease. An electric vehicle does make sound from its tires rolling down the street, but today this is masked by all the noise from the gasoline cars.

Simplicity: Electric cars have 70% fewer moving parts than internal combustion engine cars. No engine, ignition, gasoline tank, oil filter, coolant, catalytic converter, or muffler, to name a few unneeded items. There's less to go wrong, so less to service: no oil changes, no tune-ups. Some modern batteries can be expected to last the lifetime of the car. Except for attention to a few other components, like rotating the tires, there's relatively little work to be done on electric cars unless something breaks, which is uncommon. Since the regenerative braking system helps slow down the car, brakes get used less and need replacing less often. Electric motors can provide as many as 1 million miles (1.6 million km) of service.

Who wouldn't like a simpler, low-maintenance car? Today's car companies, perhaps. For auto dealers, service and parts sales made up 12% of dealer revenues in 2004, and these accounted for 57% of profits.[4] (New vehicle sales generated nearly 30% of profits, and used vehicle sales provided 13% of profits. The average dealership netted $560,000 in profit before taxes.) With electric vehicles, less servicing and fewer parts sales could wipe out a big chunk of profits; all those oil changes and tune-ups add up. In addition, independent muffler repair shops or smog-testing stations would be out of business if all cars were electric, though other businesses and jobs would sprout up centered on electric-drive technology.

It's plausible to think that one reason the automotive industry resisted the introduction of electric cars so vehemently is that it augured a radical shift in parts manufacturing and maintenance. New assembly lines would be needed for electric cars and their parts. Some parts for cars with internal combustion engines eventually might become obsolete. Combine that with a possible decline in revenues from parts and servicing, and the car company bean counters had an incentive to maintain the status quo.

Because plug-in hybrids combine electric and liquid-fuel propulsion systems, they could pose less of an economic threat to the existing auto industry.

Efficiency: Electric vehicles use less energy than gasoline vehicles. Why?

Electric drive systems are able to convert more of the available energy into the force that propels the car, thus wasting less energy and requiring less energy to go the same distance as a gasoline car. In addition, electric vehicles (as well as hybrids and plug-in hybrids) use regenerative braking to convert some of the kinetic energy of a moving vehicle to electrical energy and store it in batteries for later use. Without regenerative braking, kinetic energy is wasted as it converts to heat from friction between the brake disks and the brake pads.

By itself, an electric vehicle is four times more efficient than a similar gasoline vehicle. Factor in the energy used at the gasoline refinery or the electrical power plant, and electric vehicles remain twice as efficient as gasoline vehicles, according to the Sacramento (California) Municipal Utility District.[5]

Even if you include the "full fuel cycle," accounting for the energy used to make the fuel (electricity or gasoline), the energy losses incurred in transporting the fuel, and the energy used to run the car, electric cars still come out ahead.

One of these so-called well-to-wheels comparisons, conducted for Canadian health officials, estimated that an electric car requires only 14%–46% of the energy required by a car with an internal combustion engine, depending on the source of the electricity.[6]

Using well-to-wheels analysis to compare cars is a very complex version of "Mirror, mirror on the wall, who's the fairest of them all?" The results depend a lot on what you put into it in the first place — the assumptions that you use as the basis for the analysis. How far back do you go in calculating the energy used? Do you include the energy required to make the windmill or to build the gasoline refinery? Do you include the energy required to pump the oil out of the ground, or to mine for coal? Do you include the energy expended in wars over oil, or to clean up oil spills? Well-to-wheels analyses don't go this far, but this shows how complete comparisons remain elusive.

Despite their complexity, well-to-wheels analyses are the only fair way to compare the efficiency and emissions of different auto technologies. They show that electric cars are more efficient than gasoline cars.

The Argonne National Laboratory employs what may be the gold standard for comparing the efficiencies and emissions of car technologies and fuels, known as the Greenhouse Gases, Regulated Emissions, and Energy Use in Transportation (GREET) computer model. An Argonne study using the GREET 1.6 model estimates that a car charged by electricity from the US mix of power plants uses 46% of the amount of energy used by a car running on reformulated gasoline, or 50% of the energy if the electricity comes from California's mix of power plants, which use less coal to generate power.[7]

Put another way, the "fleet average" fuel efficiency of US gasoline cars (20 miles or 32 km per gallon) is the equivalent of 1,600–1,700 watt-hours per mile in electrical terms. A relatively chunky electric vehicle like the Toyota RAV4-EV (a small SUV) gets by with only 250–300 watt-hours per mile, or 17% of the energy required by the average gasoline vehicle, according to calculations by Nick Carter, PhD, an electric-vehicle activist in Northern California.

Using yet a different mode of comparison, another electric-vehicle activist in Southern California notes that at a fuel efficiency of 20 miles (32 km) per gallon, the average fleet car needs 5 gallons of gasoline to go 100 miles (160 km). The Toyota Prius hybrid needs 2 gallons to go that far, and the more aerodynamic Honda Insight hybrid uses 1.6 gallons to travel that 100 miles (160 km). The RAV4-EV goes 30% farther — about 130 miles (208 km) — on the energy equivalent of just 1 gallon of gasoline (34,000 watt-hours or 34kWh), and the more aerodynamic GM EV1 could go nearly 200 miles (320 km) on the same amount of energy.

Why does energy efficiency matter? A more efficient car means that you need less fuel (gasoline or electricity) made from petroleum, natural gas, or coal to drive, which reduces costs and pollution. Or a more efficient car means that you need less electricity made from wind, solar, or geothermal sources, which means fewer solar panels or windmills and less cost.

Not surprisingly, the efficiency of plug-in hybrids falls inbetween gasoline cars and electric cars. The US Department of Energy estimated that plug-in hybrids will reduce fuel use by 50% (or better) compared with gasoline cars. That means that 1.5 million plug-in hybrids on the road could save 20 million barrels of oil per year.[8]

A recent survey by the nonpartisan Civil Society Institute in Boston showed that two-thirds of Americans feel it is patriotic to buy a more fuel-efficient vehicle.[9] Even pickup truck owners, despite a stereotypical image as macho drivers who value power above all, rated fuel economy as the most important attribute of their trucks in a recent survey commissioned by the New York-based environmental advocacy group Environmental Defense. The random survey of 300 pickup truck owners found that they valued fuel economy more highly than horsepower, off-road capability, and all other attributes combined.[10]

Cost: Driving an electric car for a mile uses about the same amount of electricity as turning on a toaster or toaster oven for 10–15 minutes. It's not free, but it's not a huge chunk of change, either.

In general, driving on electricity costs 20%–50% of the cost of fueling conventional cars or hybrids because driving on electricity is more efficient and electricity is less expensive than gasoline.

TABLE 1. Comparing costs for fuel.

Vehicle	Miles (km) per gal.	Cost per mi. (km) US$
Mid-size SUV	17 (27)	15 (9) cents
Compact sedan	32 (51)	8 (5) cents
Full hybrid	50 (80)	5 (3) cents
Electric vehicle	110* (176)	2 (1.5) cents

* Per 34kWh of electricity, the energy equivalent of a gallon of gasoline.

Electricity rates vary by region and, in some cases, by the time of day if the customer employs time-of-use metering. For electric car drivers, time-of-use metering saves money because the utility charges lower rates during off-peak hours on weekends and between midnight and 7 A.M., when electric cars and plug-in hybrid cars typically get charged. Driving these kinds of cars saves money compared to driving gasoline cars.

Let's compare fuel costs using conservative numbers.[11] The average price for electricity in the United States is $.08 per kWh, but prices typically are much cheaper for off-peak electricity at night when electric vehicles plug in. Yet even if we assume that electricity costs $.08 per kWh and gasoline costs $2.50 per gallon, driving on electricity costs a lot less, as shown in Table 1.

Those pennies in difference add up. The average American drives 15,000 miles (9,375 km) each year. Fuel for one year would cost $371 for an electric vehicle, $750 for a good hybrid, $1,172 for a conventional compact sedan, and $2,206 for a conventional mid-size SUV.

The cost of fueling a plug-in hybrid, again, will fall in-between costs for electric cars and hybrids. The National Renewable Energy Laboratory modeled the savings using more conservative fuel prices of $2.15 per gallon for gasoline and $.09 per kWh for electricity. A fleet of plug-in hybrids would cut operating costs in half compared with a conventional fleet, saving approximately $600 per year for each vehicle in the fleet.[12]

In terms of cost, however, the first thing a car buyer looks at is the sticker price. In that respect, electric cars have been more expensive than most conventional cars or hybrids of the same type, mainly because they never were mass-produced. Car companies made so few of them that they essentially were hand-built, custom-made vehicles. Even then, the sticker prices of electric vehicles were lower than prices for the first Hummers and less than many luxury vehicles.

The cost of batteries also kept the cost of electric cars high, again partly because they weren't produced in sufficiently large quantities to reach a scale of production that would lower costs. Even with the added cost, however, every electric vehicle offered to the public was leased or bought, and their popularity generated waiting lists.

The mass production of hybrids, however, has started to reduce the cost of many of the electrical components "borrowed" from electric vehicles, and that trend should continue as hybrids increase in number and as plug-in hybrids hit the market. Making plug-in hybrid versions of today's cars initially will cost more upfront than either gasoline or hybrid cars because they have more batteries, but much of that extra cost would disappear if plug-in hybrids are designed from the ground up with smaller gasoline engines. Engines don't need to be as large when combined with an electric drivetrain for power.

Despite the higher initial cost of plug-in hybrids, consumers would save money. Terry Penney, manager of the National Renewable Energy Laboratory's FreedomCAR program, told attendees at a 2005 meeting of the Association for the Study of Peak Oil and Gas that he had developed a spreadsheet plotting electricity rates and gasoline prices to calculate whether consumers would pay more in the big picture for a plug-in hybrid with enough batteries for a 10-mile (16-km) all-electric range. In 45 out of 50 states (all but a few states with the highest electricity prices), a plug-in hybrid would put money in the driver's pocket because the savings in fuel would more than offset a higher sales price and the cost of batteries.[13]

Emissions: An electric car has no tailpipe because it has no emissions. Enough said. When considering pollution from the car itself, the more electric the car is, the fewer emissions it makes. Electric vehicles emit less than plug-in hybrids, which emit less than hybrids, which emit less than conventional cars. A conventional compact sedan emits approximately 320 grams (g) per mile of the greenhouse gas carbon dioxide. A plug-in hybrid would emit less than 200 g per mile, according to one estimate by the Electric Power Research Institute (EPRI), a research arm of the electrical utility industry, based in Palo Alto, California.

But the fuel, electricity, or gasoline, has to come from somewhere, and that "somewhere" usually involves some pollution. We'll take a look at full-cycle, well-to-wheel emissions in chapter 6. For now, suffice it to say that electric vehicles and plug-in hybrids produce fewer emissions than do gasoline cars or hybrids, even if you include the emissions from power plants. In addition, electric vehicles and plug-in hybrids move emissions away from large population centers, and the remaining emissions from power plants are easier to regulate than trying to control emissions from hundreds of millions of tailpipes.

Safety: Electric vehicles have proven to be as safe to drive as any other car, or safer.

Power: Modern electric vehicles have plenty of power; they don't handle like golf carts. The land speed record for electric vehicles is 245 miles (392 km) per hour. The Tzero, a sporty two-seater demonstration model created in 2000 by Southern California-based innovators AC Propulsion, can accelerate from 0 to 60 miles per hour (96 km/h) in 3.6 seconds, powered by 6,800 lithium-ion (Li-ion) battery cells wired together. (Called 18650 cells, they're the kind used in laptop computers and are slightly larger than AA-sized batteries.) An earlier version of the Tzero that used Optima recombinant lead-acid battery cells (weighing 500 pounds more and with one quarter the battery energy) still outran a Ferrari, a Porsche, a Corvette, and a Lamborghini in separate drag races. In 2006 Silicon Valley startup Wrightspeed put Li-ion batteries in a stripped-down concept car called the X1 that zoomed from 0 to 60 miles per hour (96 km/h) in three seconds. Another California startup, Tesla Motors, began selling a luxury electric roadster that could accelerate from 0 to 60 miles per hour (96 km/h) in four seconds or go 250 miles (400 km) per charge.

Range: A key factor in how far one can drive on electricity — whether in an electric car, a hybrid, or a plug-in hybrid — is the batteries.

The Tzero sportscar with lead-acid batteries driven at 60 miles (96 km) per hour had a range of 100 miles (160 km). With the more energy-dense Li-ion batteries today it goes 300 miles (320 km) per charge.

The first-generation EV1s had a purported range of 60–90 miles (96–144 km) before needing recharging. The second-generation EV1, with better nickel metal-hydride (NiMH) batteries, could go 140 miles (224 km) per charge. Similar batteries used in the larger Toyota RAV4-EV gave it a maximum range of about 125 miles (200 km). Modern nickel-metal-hydride batteries would take these vehicles even further.

That might not seem like much, but try this: Write down how many miles you drive in each car trip and keep a log for a week or two. You might be surprised at how little you actually drive. Americans average 35 miles (56 km) of travel in personal vehicles per day, the sum of four one-way trips each day, according to the 2001 National Household Travel Survey, conducted by the US Department of Transportation.[14] That would mean that the average "trip" by a car, SUV, or truck is less than 10 miles (16 km).

Averages don't necessarily reflect the driving patterns of a majority of Americans, so let's look at this another way. An earlier version of the federal survey, the 1990 Nationwide Personal Transportation Survey, found that 50% of American drivers travel 25 miles (40 km) per day or less, and 80% drive 50 miles (80 km) per day or less.[15]

Even the electric vehicle with the shortest range among those offered by the car companies — the Ford Th!nkCity — could go 35–50 miles (56–80 km) between charges, meaning it could handle 50%–80% of American driving.

A US Department of Energy study showed that a plug-in hybrid with a 10-mile all-electric range would cover 25% of average American driving in electric mode. A 25-mile electric range would cover 50% of driving before substantial use of the gasoline engine. A 45-mile electric range would cover nearly 70% of driving, then turn to gasoline.[16] And, of course, the backup gasoline engine would handle the rest of driving.

Convenience: Both electric vehicles and plug-in hybrids bring the convenience of recharging at home, typically overnight. If a driver goes further than the batteries can handle, recharging an electric car away from home can be inconvenient because the process can take several hours. With a plug-in hybrid, there's no need to think about charging anywhere but home, because the gasoline engine acts as a backup; but that does mean occasional trips to the gas station.

Batteries: The first-generation EV1s that were supposed to go 70–90 miles (112–144 km) per charge initially were offered with defective lead-acid batteries, many of which had to be recalled. Lead-acid batteries aren't necessarily defective — hobbyists and racers have been converting gasoline cars to electric cars successfully using lead-acid batteries for decades — but the particular batteries that GM chose had problems. Do-it-yourself conversions of less-aerodynamic conventional cars to electric cars typically use inexpensive lead-acid batteries and get a real-world range of 20–60 miles (32–96 km).

Even though those ranges would meet the needs of most commuters, consumers have been conditioned to demand more. Advertising-driven expectations, combined with the sorry state of mass transit in the United States, convince many drivers that they need to own a huge, four-wheel-drive, cliff-climbing monster of an SUV with an enormous gasoline tank just in case they ever need to drive 300 miles (480 km) over a snowy mountain range with six people on board. Instead, most of these SUVs rumble around cities and suburbs most of their lives.

By the late 1990s, a much better battery chemistry than lead-acid came on the market. NiMH batteries went into the second-generation EV1, the Toyota RAV4-EV, the Honda EV Plus, the electric Ford Ranger truck, the Chrysler EPIC minivan, and the electric Chevrolet S10 truck. With NiMH, the vehicles could go 80–140 miles (128–224 km), depending on the model and how fast or carefully it was driven. The Ford Th!nkCity, which was intended to be a short-distance runabout for city driving, used less expensive nickel-cadmium batteries with shorter range.

NiMH batteries changed the game. Suddenly electric vehicles were much more satisfying to people. Unfortunately, they made a late debut, coming on the scene just as automakers were shutting down their electric-vehicle programs, convinced that they could defeat the ZEV Mandate. Luckily, enough NiMH batteries made it into vehicles and built up an impressive track record. The investor-owned utility Southern California Edison, which had over 320 vehicles in probably the largest electric-vehicle fleet in the nation, extensively tested NiMH batteries in Toyota RAV4-EVs. The company put them through torture tests, running the electric SUVs in hot temperatures, without air conditioning to cool the batteries, and charging the batteries with fairly high charge resistance, meaning they generate a lot of heat while charging. Utility drivers racked up more than 100,000 miles (160,000 km) on some cars. Still the batteries maintained good performance and durability, suggesting that they would last through 150,000 miles (240,000 km) of driving, which traditionally is considered the lifespan of motor vehicles.

Battery researchers continued to make improvements, but companies never began the large-scale production of NiMH batteries for electric vehicles that would bring their cost down.

One of the world's largest oil companies may have played a role in that decision: ChevronTexaco.

In 1994 GM bought a controlling interest in Energy Conversion Devices (ECD), the company that invented the Ovonic NiMH batteries used in the electric vehicles and that held the battery patents. GM sold its interest to Texaco (which later merged with Chevron). ECD and ChevronTexaco formed an equal partnership in the spinoff battery company, now called Cobasys. When Toyota began using a better version of NiMH batteries made by Panasonic EV Energy in its RAV4-EV, ECD sued for patent infringement. Its parent company, Cobasys, entered into a confidential settlement with the Japanese companies in July, 2004.

In 2005 Cobasys granted Panasonic EV Energy a license to sell NiMH batteries "for certain North American transportation applications," for which Cobasys will receive royalties until 2015, federal reports filed by Cobasys show. In recent years, the only NiMH batteries sold for vehicles in North America by any company have been for hybrids — cars that must use the petroleum products that make up Chevron's core business. Plug-in hybrids and electric vehicles ideally use bigger batteries than the versions in hybrids.

It's possible that Cobasys is squelching all access to large NiMH batteries through its control of patent licenses in order to remove a competitor to gasoline. Or it's possible that Cobasys, which also makes and sells the batteries, simply wants the market for itself and is waiting for a major automaker to start producing plug-in hybrids or electric vehicles.

Because the battle over NiMH patent infringement occurred at the same time that automakers were winning the fight to destroy California's ZEV Mandate and shutting their already minimal electric-vehicle programs, it's impossible to tell whether the larger NiMH batteries disappeared due to licensing restrictions or because the electric-vehicle market collapsed.

The Cobasys battery plant in Springboro, Ohio, that opened in 2003, is capable of making millions of NiMH batteries per year. Will Cobasys sell any that are larger than the NiMH batteries used in hybrids? Only time — and the market for plug-in hybrids — will tell.

Hybrids have captured the market's attention since the murder of the ZEV Mandate. But automakers used a much more exotic technology to help kill the Mandate — hydrogen fuel-cell vehicles.

THE TECH SQUAD

CHAPTER 3

Felix Flirts with Hydrogen

FELIX KRAMER TOOK the piece of copper pipe and a hammer onto the driveway outside the crowded garage of Ron Gremban's townhouse. It was too cramped in there for Kramer's six-foot, two-inch frame, what with all the tools and random but useful pieces of materials and dozens of carefully labeled boxes and drawers full of parts and supplies. Plus too many "cooks" were stirring the pot they were focused on — converting Gremban's silver 2004 Toyota Prius into a plug-in hybrid. They would make it a Prius *plus* more batteries and a plug for recharging, so they dubbed it the PRIUS+.

Their modifications would allow the car to get 100 miles (160 km) per gallon of gasoline plus a bit of cheap electricity. The PRIUS+ would show the world that these cars could be made today. If a bunch of hackers could do it in Gremban's garage, surely Toyota or one of the other car companies could make much better plug-in hybrids now, instead of waiting for the holy grail of hydrogen fuel-cell cars that they all were promising.

The PRIUS+ would be an improvement, but there's no denying what a great car they had to start from. Toyota had built an impressive product: complex; efficient, and low-polluting. It seamlessly coordinated gasoline and electric drivetrains with an advanced computer control system. Kramer imagined how Toyota engineers might be aghast at what they now were attempting — messing with the management system, adding batteries and a charger.

The project would take engineering skill, a mind for electronics, and the know-how to write computer code to fool the Prius system. It would take someone who could scope out the right batteries and components, or hand-make the components if necessary. It would take someone who could troubleshoot dozens of mechanical, electrical, and computer glitches.

That someone was not Kramer.

He squinted in the sun outside the beige row of condos and knelt down to place the copper pipe on the warm black pavement. Holding it steady with one hand, he swung back the hammer, gave the pipe a good, hard whack, then kept on pounding. The ringing sounds of metal on metal echoed those from Marc Geller, who pounded another length of copper pipe next to Kramer on the driveway. Their job: smash those suckers flat. Then pick up another piece of pipe, and smash it flat too. And another.

Although Kramer was the founder and lead strategist of the California Cars Initiative, known as CalCars, he was happy today to be taking orders from CalCars' lead technical coordinator, Ron Gremban. The two of them were the figureheads of CalCars, heading up a virtual community of engineers, entrepreneurs, and activists who had spent months preparing for this day. Gremban knew in his head what needed to happen and the basics of how to do most of it. He didn't have a written list or instructions. When a volunteer was free, he offered a task. If the volunteer's skills weren't up to the task, he gently offered a simpler one.

Gremban had helped build an electric car once and worked for a short time in the 1970s for a small electric-car company, directing research and development. But that was decades ago. Since then he'd moved into software development and sales of solar energy systems. For this project, he was relying on his research, his smarts, and an invaluable collection of electric-vehicle enthusiasts who communicated mainly by e-mail and Web postings.

They had worked out much of the plans and specifications online together. When the parts were delivered and the time came for action, Kramer posted a call in September, 2004, to volunteers all over the San Francisco Bay Area to come by Gremban's Corte Madera condo whenever they could help.

Volunteers showed up every day for two weeks, usually two or three a day. Only a few had specialized skills; mostly they just had enthusiasm. Their initiative and cleverness amazed Gremban. He didn't have time to worry about whether they would succeed; there was too much to do to bother thinking about that. "There was so much happening so fast that it had to happen organically," he recalled.

Someone picked up the stray aluminum strips in Gremban's garage and made a box to house the batteries. Someone else cut plywood to fit under the battery box. They bent plastic for a plenum and installed fans to cool the batteries. They mounted contactors, lots of homemade circuit boards, a fuse block, and a terminal strip. In the driver's compartment, near the dashboard they drilled and installed an analogue meter that would help assess the PRIUS+ performance once it got going. All the cables and connectors needed lugs put on their ends. There was a seemingly endless amount of point-to-point wiring needed for the coils and contactors and fans and other parts. The less-skilled volunteers made repeated runs to the local big-box hardware store for supplies.

They improvised when needed: wrapping aluminum foil around a toroid to form a Faraday cage to isolate it from electrical fields, and covering it with a plastic bag to isolate it further so that it wouldn't short out something.

An online advisor with relatively recent experience converting a gasoline car to electric had warned Gremban that he'd need flexibility in the wiring between the batteries, or else the contacts would work loose due to the vibration while driving. The normal solution — cables — wouldn't fit in the tight space of the Prius hatchback's battery box and would be too much work anyway. Another solution — busbars — typically would be too rigid. That's where the copper tubing came in handy. Flattened, bent,

California Cars Initiative (CalCars).

Ron Gremban, Felix Kramer, Marc Geller, Kevin Lyons, and Andrew Lawton work on the first PRIUS+.

and attached to the battery contacts, they had enough spring in them to absorb the vibrations.

Kramer, Geller, and Kevin Lyons pounded tube after tube of copper. Andrew Lawton took the flattened strips, bent them into busbars, and positioned them between the rows of batteries sitting in the back of the Prius, above the spare-tire well and below the removable floorboard.

Kramer paused in his pounding to rest, and marveled at the five volunteers assembled here. This would go down in history as one of the largest meetings of CalCars' members. A historian at heart, Kramer liked to think of his days as being full of historical moments, on the optimistic assumption that the events will be of significance to the future. There was some precedence for this — the Lawrence Felix Kramer Archive at Cornell University, his alma mater, includes a year's worth of leaflets and buttons that he collected at college and during a year that he took off from school to do anti-Viet Nam War and anti-draft organizing.

The same impulses led him to save every e-mail in a complete CalCars archive and to make the whole endeavor as open-source as possible, sharing everything for free with anyone who might be interested. CalCars was a light, lean non-profit that achieved its goals primarily through electronic communications, virtual community, and "viral networking."

Kramer stood up and pushed his smudged glasses back up the bridge of his nose. Though he was a sometime-marathon runner and in good shape, crouching and hammering was hard work. He stepped into the shade of the garage and entered the side door to the condo, his head nearly even with the carpeted catwalk that Gremban had built for his kitties, trailing along the top of the wall from the garage, down a hall, and into the kitchen. Kramer poured himself a cold glass of water and looked out over the grassy creekbed beside the townhouse complex, framed by the sounds of rushing cars on the freeway nearby.

Water and cars. This whole thing, in a way, had started with water and cars.

HYDROGEN HEATS UP

Water is one part oxygen and two parts hydrogen. Hydrogen is attached to lots of elements in the universe but doesn't exist alone naturally. For ages inventors have toyed with ways to pry hydrogen loose and use the extremely combustible gas as fuel.

One of those hydrogen visionaries had been a role model for Kramer: Amory Lovins, founder of the environmental think tank The Rocky Mountain Institute, whose articles about alternative energy influenced Kramer's thinking in the late 1970s. Twenty years later, Kramer, a successful entrepreneur, picked up a 1999 book co-authored by Lovins, *Natural Capitalism*. The authors posited a vast array of ecologically smart options available to businesses and devoted a whole chapter to describing the Hypercar, an ultralight, aerodynamic vehicle fueled by hybrid hydrogen-electric systems that emitted nothing but a trickle of water.

The idea caught Kramer's fancy at just the right time; he was ready for a change in his life. One of the earliest desktop publishers in the 1980s, he wrote the first book about this field in 1990, self-produced and self-marketed, of course. That was the first time he sold a product that he believed in, and he learned how savvy marketing to user groups in the pre-Internet days could lead to sales. By 1994 he was doing Internet marketing of other people's products.

Kramer sold his desktop publishing business in 1997 when he and his wife, Rochelle Lefkowitz, and their son Josh moved to Northern California from New York City. Over the next four years he built an online business, eConstructors.com, a market-place of Web developers. He raised $1 million in angel financing during the Silicon Valley boom years and sold the successful business in early 2001, just after the high-flying, high-tech economy went bust. It didn't make him rich, but between that and a few profits from stock investments, he had the luxury of deciding just what he wanted to do next. For a time, at least, he could do whatever he wanted.

What called to him was one of his first loves — environmentalism. As a college student, he had experienced the first Earth Day in 1970. He realized early on that prices of goods in our economy don't reflect their full cost because they seldom include the costs to the environment.

He became executive director of New York SunDay, part of a broader solar energy day with events around the country, during which President Jimmy Carter put solar collectors on the White House. (President Ronald Reagan took them down, and President George W. Bush put them back up.) The small group behind New York SunDay created a professional-looking brochure for a solar trade show, with a picture on the cover of the massive US Custom House (now the Museum of American Indians) "to show that we were real. We didn't have any exhibitors yet," Kramer recalled. The brochure projected a vision and described how to make it real. "That's been kind of my guiding principle ever since," he said. "It has worked well to say to people, 'Here's where we want to be. Here's what we aim to do. Here's what we've got now.'"

Later he worked as executive director of a non-profit organization that merged environmental technology with urban social justice issues. In the Reagan era, as the price of oil dropped, support for alternative energy waned. Computers came on the scene, and Kramer wandered away from his environmental roots, at least professionally.

In 2001 he was a free man with some money, and here was the Hypercar (or at least the idea of it) being championed by one of his heroes. "It was just amazing, and sounded like it was real," he recalled. Surely now was the time to follow his heart and become a green entrepreneur. He approached Hypercar, which the Rocky Mountain Institute had spun off as a business, with the idea of taking advance orders for the car in California instead of simply waiting for the major automakers to become interested.

Kramer had another reason that year to follow his dreams. Ever since he was a teenager, he'd gradually been losing his hearing and developed tinnitus (ringing in the ears). Now things were getting much worse. Medical imaging showed an acoustic neuroma — a benign tumor on one ear canal. Before undergoing the lengthy, near-brain surgery to remove the tumor, he took a vacation to Europe with his family that he'd been postponing for years.

Surgeons said removing the tumor was like scraping peanut butter off of a wet noodle. It left him with no hearing in one ear and wrecked much of his vestibular function, his sense of balance. Riding a bike or ice-skating became harder, but he could still run and ski.

It all made Kramer think hard about what he wanted to do. What he could do.

A year of discussions with Hypercar didn't lead to much, so Kramer made an adjustment. He would start a business that would take orders for future delivery of the ultralight, fully optimized hydrogen fuel-cell cars and then hire Hypercar to make them. With co-sponsorship from Hypercar, he invited 75 engineers, environmentalists, and investors who were familiar with the Hypercar concept to a meeting at the knOwhere Store in Palo Alto, California, to found the California Car Company Initiative.

The concept of hydrogen fuel-cell cars was hot. "It enchanted me and a lot of other people," Kramer said. The idea seemed appealing. Hydrogen is the most abundant element in the universe. The process would use electricity to strip hydrogen from its tight bond with other elements in natural gas or water. Later the hydrogen would be combined with oxygen on the electrode of a fuel cell in a car, generating electricity that would then run the electric car. Out the tailpipe would come nothing but trickles of water.

When scientists managed to cut the cost of a particular kind of fuel cell by nearly a factor of 10 in the early 1990s, they sparked a conflagration of interest in fuel-cell research, especially for transportation. Auto companies, oil companies, and new industries jumped on board. GM, Honda, Toyota, DaimlerChrysler, Nissan, and Hyundai each began spending hundreds of millions of dollars on fuel-cell vehicle research and development.

German automaker Daimler-Benz declared in 1997 that it would start selling a minimum of 100,000 hydrogen fuel-cell vehicles by 2005.[1] Ford said it would have a prototype to show by 2000. Later in 1997, Ford formed a joint venture with Daimler-Benz and Ballard Power Systems, saying they expected to have fuel-cell vehicles on the road by 2004. After the 1998 merger that produced DaimlerChrysler, the company revised its estimates to 40,000 fuel-cell vehicles in 2004 and 100,000 in 2006. In November 2000, DaimlerChrysler unveiled its Necar 5 fuel-cell vehicle. Spokesmen admitted the fuel cell was still in the development stage but felt it could be competitive with the internal combustion engine in a few years.[2]

In July 2000, GM introduced a prototype fuel-cell vehicle called the HydroGen1 and predicted it would be competitive in showrooms by 2004. GM and Toyota announced that they would work together on hydrogen fuel-cell research, and Honda said it was spending millions of dollars to develop its own fuel-cell vehicles. Ford, DaimlerChrysler, and Ballard teamed up with oil companies Texaco, ARCO, and Shell and the State of California to form "The California Fuel Cell Partnership: Driving for the Future," which still exists today.

In his 2003 State of the Union address, President George W. Bush proposed funding $1.2 billion in research on "clean, hydrogen-powered automobiles." Two months later, the California Air Resources Board (CARB) chose the promises of future hydrogen-powered cars over the reality of electric cars and essentially took the "zero" out of the Zero Emission Vehicles Mandate.

CARB's Alan Lloyd preferred to switch rather than fight the car companies. "They're all working on fuel-cell vehicles. And that didn't happen with battery electrics. So to me, that is the huge difference," he would later tell filmmakers.[3]

General Motors officials in August of 2003 argued that changes in federal fuel-efficiency regulations should be delayed because the promise of hydrogen cars was about to be fulfilled. By 2004, the GM-Toyota cooperation on fuel cells had dissolved, and Toyota all but abandoned the hydrogen scenario, while saying in public that it was keeping all options open.

Toyota's spokesman Bill Reinert admitted in media interviews that "the cars have a limited range, the durability of the cars isn't so very good, and they don't do well in cold weather. Other than that, they're great." For saying that it might be 20 to 30 years before consumers could go to a dealer and get one, he took flak from federal and state officials and people in the hydrogen industry. "Just because a lot of people want it to work is no guarantee," Reinert said.

HYDROGEN DEFLATED

Toyota had banked primarily on hybrids, so disparaging statements about hydrogen could be tinged with self-interest. But the company was far from alone in waving warning flags about hydrogen hype.

Joseph J. Romm, a former energy official in the Clinton administration, posits five "miracles" that must take place for hydrogen fuel-cell cars to be competitive. The cars cost about $1 million each, so that's got to drop. Because hydrogen is so light, there is no known material that can hold enough of the gas, even if condensed under pressure, to give a car the kind of range consumers want, so designing on-board storage seems impossible. The cost of making hydrogen would need to decrease by at least two- or three-fold, probably more. Tens of thousands of expensive hydrogen fueling stations would need to be erected before anyone knows whether the cars will succeed on the marketplace. And competing car technologies must not look like better options than hydrogen fuel-cell vehicles.

Plug-in hybrid technology already seems superior to hydrogen fuel-cell cars on a number of levels and is available sooner, he adds.

Romm served in the Department of Energy during a nearly 10-fold buildup in funding for research on hydrogen fuel cells from 1993 to 1998. Research advances steadily reduced the cost of fuel cells, but they remained extremely expensive, and the other limitations of hydrogen-powered transportation couldn't be ignored. By 2004 Romm was touring to promote his book, *The Hype About Hydrogen: Fact and Fiction in the Race to Save the Climate* (Island Press, 2004), and decrying the huge amounts of money being squandered on hydrogen programs instead of funding plug-in hybrids and other technologies that could make a difference much sooner.

Romm has called the hydrogen scenario "one of the biggest blunders in the history of the automotive industry."

Hydrogen is the tiniest and leakiest of gas molecules and much more flammable than natural gas or gasoline. Cellphones can ignite a hydrogen fire, which burns almost invisibly. People have been known to walk into hydrogen fires because they don't see them.

The only fossil fuel-free scenario for a hydrogen economy depends on using electricity from renewable sources to separate water into hydrogen and oxygen by electrolysis, an extremely energy-intensive process. It would require as much electricity as was sold in all of 2004 to make enough hydrogen to power half of the US vehicles in 2025.[4]

The basic inefficiency of hydrogen vehicles is simple to describe. Here's the loop for an electric car: Electricity is stored in batteries, then used to power the car. Here's the loop for a hydrogen car: Electricity is used to make the hydrogen, which is combined with oxygen on board the car to make electricity, which then powers what basically is an electric car.

Multiple analyses report that three or four times as much electricity would be needed to run a car on hydrogen compared with using the electricity directly in an electric car to go the same distance. That's because after using electricity to create hydrogen through electrolysis, transporting the hydrogen, pumping it, and converting it back to electricity in a fuel cell, only 20%–25% of the original electricity reaches the motor, Romm explained.[5] In an electric car, 75%–80% of the original electricity reaches the motor after transmission through the electrical grid, charging the car's batteries and discharging the batteries. Electric cars and plug-in hybrids should be able to run in electric mode three to four times the distance of a hydrogen fuel-cell car on the same amount of electricity.

One study calculated a smaller difference and says that if wind power is used to generate electricity, 60% more windmills would be needed to run a car on hydrogen compared with running an electric car.[6]

Whether the difference is 60% or 300%–400%, using the electricity directly in electric vehicles and plug-in hybrids makes more sense than squandering it on hydrogen production. Why build 160–400 windmills when 100 would suffice?

For example, the Canadian province of Manitoba gets nearly all of its electricity from renewables, mainly from hydroelectric dams. The existing power capacity at night there already is sufficient to power all vehicles in the province if they were battery-electric, but hydrogen cars would require the building of two more large dams producing over 1,000 mW each, Manitoba Hydro's Ed Innes said at a 2005 meeting of the Electric Drive Transportation Association.

AC Propulsion, a Southern California research and design company for electric vehicles, compared the 2003 Honda FCX fuel-cell vehicle (a sedan) with the 2003 Toyota RAV4-EV electric SUV (a compact SUV). To go one mile, the Honda FCX requires 1.2kWh of electricity, while the RAV4-EV needs only 0.3kWh, making the electric SUV four times more efficient than the fuel-cell car.

Fuel-cell vehicles won't necessarily reduce greenhouse gas emissions, either. AC Propulsion's Alec Brooks (now with Aero-Vironment) compared the Honda FCX to the conventional Honda Civic gasoline car. Assuming that 33% of the electricity used to make the hydrogen comes from new sources of emission-free renewable energy (like solar or wind power) and the rest comes from the relatively clean California electricity grid, the Honda FCX still would produce more global-warming gases than would the gasoline Honda Civic: 341 grams of carbon dioxide per mile with hydrogen versus 321 grams per mile with gasoline.

The renewable energy used to make hydrogen would have a better environmental impact if instead it was fed to the grid to reduce the need for energy from less-clean sources and the associated power plant emissions. Brooks' analysis suggests that if we combine this reduction in emissions with the amount of emissions produced by the gasoline Civic, the overall carbon dioxide per mile would be lowered to 153 grams per mile. Replace the Civic with a Prius hybrid in that scenario, and the carbon dioxide total drops to 30 grams per mile.

The numbers get into the negative range when substituting electric-drive cars for the Civic. Feeding the renewable energy to the grid and driving a plug-in Prius would result in an overall decrease of 6 grams per mile of carbon dioxide because more emissions are avoided from the grid than are produced by the car. Send the renewable energy to the grid and drive a Toyota RAV4-EV, which has no emissions, and 27 grams per mile of carbon dioxide are avoided.

Using renewable energy to reduce the need for coal-fired electricity would prevent three times as many greenhouse gases as using the renewable energy to run cars on hydrogen fuel cells, a study by the Institute for Lifecycle Environmental Assessment concluded.[7] The number of solar panels needed to power a hydrogen fuel-cell car for a day could power an electric car plus run a house for a day if the electricity is fed to the grid, AC Propulsion estimated.

In 2003 electric-vehicle activist Mike Kane calculated the number of solar panels needed to make electricity for an electric Honda EV Plus driving 75 miles (120 km) per day. He compared that with panels needed to power a Stuart Energy Hydrogen generator to run a Honda FCX fuel-cell car the same distance. (The two cars have the same body type.) Solar panels for the electric vehicle would cost $33,600 and fill 450 square feet, meaning they would fit on the roof of an average home. Panels for the fuel-cell vehicle would cost $81,600 and fill 1,100 square feet, too expensive and too large for the average homeowner.

Then there's the unimaginable expense of a hydrogen economy. Building enough infrastructure to service 40% of US cars, light trucks, and SUVs would cost more than $500 billion, even with improved technology, one study estimated.[8] A hydrogen economy could require $2 trillion to $3 trillion just for the new pipelines to hold the hydrogen, suggested Surya Prakash, professor of chemistry at the University of South California.[9] Hydrogen fuel for just 2% of US cars would cost $20 billion, one oil company estimated.[10]

Some 50 million tons (45 million metric tons) of hydrogen is now produced worldwide for industrial uses each year, so there already is some infrastructure, Larry D. Burns, GM's director of strategic planning, noted in 2005. To construct 12,000 hydrogen filling stations in the 100 largest US cities would cost $12 billion, or $1 million per station, he estimated.[11]

In the best-case scenario, it will take decades to transition to a hydrogen economy, which *might* bring only minor reductions in carbon dioxide emissions and oil imports during the next 25 years, a National Academy of Sciences panel concluded in 2004.[12]

Despite the enthusiastic hype for hydrogen, the obvious obstacles are beginning to change some minds. By early 2006, some government officials were starting to speak truth to hydrogen, even in the presence of President Bush. Asked to describe the feasibility of hydrogen-powered transportation during a presidential visit to the National Renewable Energy Laboratory, the lab's Dale Gardner responded, "It's going to be out in the middle of the century. It's not going to be something that's going to happen in the next 15 or 20 years."

FELIX SHIFTS FOCUS

Some of the people who joined Kramer at the knOwhere Store in July of 2002 already had a sense that the hydrogen scenario might be running on hype. They gave him two key pieces of advice: make CalCars a non-profit instead of a for-profit organization, and don't bet on something so far out in the future, something so dependent on unproven technology as hydrogen fuel cells. They counseled him to focus on hybrids. Kramer listened. He dropped

"Company" and renamed the organization the California Cars Initiative (CalCars), and started looking for something to promote that was near-term, not decades away.

He was nothing if not pragmatic. Kramer had lived without a car easily for 25 years in New York, but when he came to California, he needed two cars: a sedan and a minivan for himself and his family. He checked the top-sellers and bought a Toyota Camry and a Dodge Caravan.

A few years later, he saw the EV1, but wasn't tempted to buy one. He liked the car but didn't think it had much of a future. "I always thought electric vehicles were never going to go anywhere because Americans were never going to go for a car that didn't have a longer range. All the advertising was about freedom," Kramer says.

In late 2002 an acquaintance invited him to visit the Palo Alto-based Electric Power Research Institute (EPRI) for a special event featuring the EV1 and a prototype plug-in hybrid converted from a Chevrolet Suburban SUV by a professor at the University of California, Davis.

Seeing and riding in the plug-in Suburban was a "Eureka!" moment for Kramer. "I was just amazed," he recalled. Here was the entirely pragmatic compromise between hybrids and electric vehicles — a car that could run the first 60 miles (96 km) on electricity but had a downsized internal combustion engine to provide insurance for long-distance driving.

CalCars began laying plans to convert a compact SUV into a plug-in hybrid, starting from either a Hyundai Santa Fe or a Toyota RAV4 (two compact SUVs that also had been built as electric vehicles). Kramer rejected the idea of modifying a Prius after reading articles by Toyota engineers emphasizing the impracticality of converting the first US Prius model to be a plug-in. There wasn't room for the batteries, they said, and the electrical components were sized to run only at low speeds.

Kramer went back to EPRI to talk with staff who headed up the industry research group's efforts around plug-in hybrids. EPRI had been a booster of electric vehicles in the 1990s, but its transportation division had shifted focus in 2000 in face of the automakers' staunch opposition to the Zero-Emission Vehicle (ZEV) Mandate. EPRI felt it couldn't justify spending the electrical utilities' money on a product that wasn't going to be built. Instead it formed the Hybrid Electric Vehicle Working Group to lay the groundwork for plug-in hybrids. The Working Group — comprised of representatives from the auto industry, electrical utilities, US Department of Energy, California Energy Commission, and university researchers — conducted several key studies that reported on the feasibility, benefits, and costs of plug-in hybrids.

The EPRI folks didn't quite know what to make of Kramer. Who was he, anyway? EPRI's main focus was on getting the automakers and state and federal governments to adopt plug-in hybrids. It wasn't interested in conversions, and Kramer's ideas of approaching other constituencies besides major automakers didn't mesh with EPRI's strategy. The EPRI staff was cordial but cool.

They did, however, invite him to what turned out to be the last meeting of the Hybrid Electric Vehicle Working Group. There Kramer asked a question of Toyota's chief hybrid engineer, Dave Hermance, and his answer threw Kramer for a loop.

Kramer had learned a big fancy word in talking with car people — "homologation." It encompasses all the processes needed to get government approval for a car: the crash testing, emissions testing, and meeting government specifications for all facets of the car down to the location of the interior light bulbs. The time-consuming homologation can cost auto companies tens or even hundreds of millions of dollars for each new car and is a factor that inhibits new competitors to the established automakers. Homologation for a car that's really a conversion of an existing car can be simpler, because only certain steps need to be repeated.

Kramer asked Hermance how long it would take Toyota to complete homologation if the company made a plug-in version of one of its hybrids. His answer: less than a year.

Clearly, plug-in hybrids could be on the road soon if the major automakers simply chose to make them. Kramer began monitoring the online Prius discussion groups. When he learned that the 2004 Prius would include a hatchback, a more powerful electric motor (50kW instead of 30kW), and smaller but more powerful nickel-metal hydride (NiMH) batteries (1,300W/kg instead of 1,100W/kg), he pulled every string that he could at local dealers to get on the waiting list for one of the new cars. He also ordered a custom license plate: PLUG OK.

The arrival in late 2003 of the 2004 Prius electrified the listserv postings. This second-generation US model would seal the car's status as the hybrid to beat. It became the hottest car around, generating mountains of publicity that gave Toyota a green aura. For more than a year it topped *The Wall Street Journal's* "Days on the Lot" list, reflecting how quickly the cars flew off dealers' lots.

The first thing that many owners did with the new Prius was to open it up to see how it was built. They found plenty of space for extra batteries. "It was staring you right in the face," Kramer recalled.

And then there was the button. Within days of the first 2004 models being sold, American drivers noticed a blank button on the dashboard that didn't seem to do anything. The operating manual didn't explain it. The online Prius discussion groups learned from drivers outside the United States that the button functioned in the cars sold in Europe and Japan as an "EV" mode button, allowing the car to run as an electric vehicle for a short distance. Toyota made the button inoperable in the United States because it created a problem with government regulators who knew that current smog tests couldn't accurately measure emissions from a car that could run on electricity alone at the push of a button. Devising an agreeable emissions-testing system would take time, so Toyota disabled the button to allow sales to proceed in the meantime.

By early 2004 a Texas engineer had wired his button back to life, and the buzz on the listservs ramped up. He added a 7.2-Ah lead-acid battery in parallel with the hybrid's NiMH battery. It allowed him to drive more than 2 miles (3.2 km) on electricity alone. On one cold Sunday morning (34°F), he drove a mile to the store, chatted for 45 minutes, drove a mile home, and then 5 hours later drove 17 miles (27 km) to church. With those kinds of short trips, normally he would get about 41 miles (66 km) per gallon, but with the new setup he got 53 miles (85 km) per gallon, a 32% improvement in efficiency, and avoided two out of three cold starts to the internal combustion engine. (Starting a cold engine is a prime source of pollution.) "I am so ecstatic about the possibilities here!" he wrote.

Soon after, others adapted his instructions into an online manual that Kramer helped polish and hosted on the CalCars website with photos and instructions for enabling the Prius EV button. Some Prius owners went as far as ordering the original part from Japan, so that "EV" would light up on the button when the electric-only mode was on. People started adding batteries. Kramer and others began advocating for adding a plug to the Prius. In April 2004 CalCars formally announced its plans to convert a Prius to a PRIUS+.

Ron Gremban read about CalCars' plans in the online journal *EV World* and joined in. For Kramer, Gremban was the right person in the right place at the right time. Gremban lived an hour's drive north of Kramer in the San Francisco Bay Area. Gremban had the skills and enough free time to handle the technical end of things. He too had been thinking of converting a Prius. "I enticed him to get involved more and more, to his pleasure and regret," Kramer said.

During its first three years of existence, supported by a few grants and many small donations to keep the organization going, Kramer and Gremban seldom drew a salary, donating their time in the belief that the project could change the world, and might eventually make them a living.

For Gremban as well as Kramer, this was a returning to his roots, in a sense. He and two classmates at the California Institute of Technology were the first people to drive across the United States in an electric vehicle, in the summer of 1968. Led by Wally Rippel, now with AeroVironment, the team won the race in a converted Volkswagen microbus, beating a team from the Massachusetts Institute of Technology driving a converted Chevrolet Corvair. Both cars broke down along the way, but the

VW team repaired their vehicle and crossed the finish line under electric power after nine days on the road.

Now Gremban had a Prius to play with. "This is a *much* better car," he said happily. With modern batteries, computer skills, and the Prius hybrid platform, he felt confident that they could make an exceptional car to demonstrate what the car companies could be offering to customers, if only they would.

In the next two years, the plug-in Prius that Kramer and Gremban and the tiny CalCars crew worked on that day would be featured in stories that appeared in all the major media, generating months and months of coverage. By February of 2006, a photo of Gremban's car with its GAS OPT plate peeking out from the tight fit of his garage would grace the White House website. President George W. Bush — a former oil man who let petroleum industry lobbyists craft his energy policy and embraced the hydrogen hype — would hit the road giving speech after speech praising the coming of plug-in hybrids.

The car would capture the public's imagination. But first they had to build it.

CHAPTER 4

A Small Army of Engineers

K RAMER, GREMBAN, and the California Cars Initiative (CalCars) put plug-in hybrids on the map, but they were hardly the first to make one. They followed in the footsteps of countless others whose places in history are obscured by the fact that, until the last year or two, any kind of hybrid vehicle was called simply a hybrid, whether it plugged in or relied on a gasoline engine to charge the batteries.

Hybrid vehicles started appearing in small numbers more than 100 years ago. It's reasonable to assume that many, if not most, could be plugged in. Electric cars were as numerous as gasoline cars in the early days, but specific descriptions of plugability are scarce in the literature.

The Vendovelli & Priestly three-wheeled carriage, sold in 1898, was an electric vehicle with a 40-mile (64-km) range, but for longer trips a portable 308-pound (140-kg) engine-generator could be added.[1] Several "range-extender" prototypes were designed in which an electric car pulled a trailer with an engine-generator, such as one by Linear Alpha Inc. of Evanston, Illinois,[2] in the 1970s and another by Southern California's AC Propulsion in the 1990s. The Silver Volt petro-electric car by

Aronson's Electric Fuel Propulsion Company in 1982 was a "multiple-fuel" demonstration vehicle that could fast-charge its batteries to 80% full in 45 minutes if plugged into a 220-volt, 200-amp source of electricity.[3]

Plug-in hybrid projects came and went, their builders disappearing or moving on to other technology. One of them stayed the course, however — a gentle visionary, a relatively obscure academic with a ready giggle who already had built more than a dozen plug-in hybrids, most of them with impressive 60-mile or greater all-electric ranges. Unfortunately, hardly anyone outside the auto industry noticed.

As a young faculty member at the University of Wisconsin, Andrew A. Frank and his students built his first plug-in hybrid in 1972 for a student competition. It was too far ahead of its time to work well; the technology wasn't ready. Primitive lead-acid batteries went into the car. What can be done today with electronics, he did then with mechanical widgets; he built a mechanical computer, for example.

Now a professor of mechanical and aeronautical engineering at the University of California, Davis, Frank and his students have built a new plug-in parallel hybrid almost every other year for nearly the past 20 years, each one of them for contests sponsored by the US Department of Energy, which provided some funding. Most were conversions of gasoline-only vehicles to plug-in hybrids; a few were vehicles built from the ground up. "Those were real undertakings," he says modestly, punctuating it with his trademark laugh.

One person who did notice Frank's work in the early 1990s was Dean Taylor of Southern California Edison (SCE). He steadily stoked interest in plug-in hybrids and electric vehicles for the next decade among utility colleagues and just about anybody else who would listen.

Other universities toyed with plug-in hybrids for the student competitions. The University of Illinois at Urbana-Champaign team converted a Ford Escort into a plug-in hybrid for a 1993 competition.[4] A converted Ford Taurus that used 15kWh of nickel-metal hydride (NiMH) batteries went 70 electric miles

(112 km) and got over 50 miles (80 km) per gallon of gasoline, capturing second place in a 1996 competition for the student team at Lawrence Technological University of Southfield, Michigan.

The Los Angeles Department of Water and Power briefly pursued a plug-in hybrid prototype. Frustrated with the slow pace of the major automakers in meeting the Zero-Emission Vehicle (ZEV) Mandate in the early 1990s, Los Angeles city officials sought bids from any companies that could design a clean car capable of driving on freeways. A Swedish company, Clean Air Transport, won with the LA 301, a four-seater with a 57-hp electric motor, 18kWh of batteries, a 650-cc internal combustion engine, and a 7-gallon gasoline tank. For long-distance driving, the gasoline engine augmented electric power at speeds greater than 30 mph (50 km/h), giving it a range of 150 miles (240 km) and ultra-low emissions. The Water and Power Department hoped to help make and sell 1,000 of them in 1993, but problems integrating the gasoline engine and a lack of sufficient funding spelled the end of the LA 301.[5]

Until this century, plug-in hybrids stayed on the periphery of the electric-vehicle action. "People were fixated on electric-vehicle technologies" in the 1990s, said Tien Duong, PhD, a team leader in vehicular technologies at the US Department of Energy (DOE) in Washington, DC. "We've changed," he added in 2006, "[A plug-in hybrid] is the most viable technology. I just don't know why it took us so long to think about it."

Frank pitched plug-in hybrids to all the major car companies, but they weren't interested. Too complicated, they said, or, too costly. "We've shown time and again that's not true," Frank counters. A bit more computer power replaces most of a conventional drivetrain's moving parts, making plug-in hybrids simpler, not more complex. Fewer parts and a smaller gasoline engine will offset the cost of electrical components once they're mass-produced. "We see no reason in the world why the cost of these cars needs to be higher than a conventional car" once assembly lines get rolling, Frank says.

New technology always costs more at first, so the first few plug-in hybrids to roll off assembly lines might cost 10% to 15%

more than hybrids, but that differential should drop quickly with ramped-up production. The up-front cost of the first plug-in hybrids may cost consumers an extra $4,000–$6,000 above the cost of a conventional car (or $2,000–$3,000 more than a hybrid) until prices come down with volume, Frank estimates. He shakes his head at critics' suggestion that owners may not recoup those costs in fuel savings over the life of the car. "That's what some people pay for a sunroof, leather seats, and a fancy navigation system," but they don't try to justify those purchases down to the penny, he notes. The car companies questioned his data and his calculations. "It was very hard for me to convince any major automaker that this was even a reasonable idea," mainly because they were so unfamiliar with electric-drive technology, he says.

Frank walks visitors through his warehouse lab, pointing out plug-in hybrid conversions from family sedans to large SUVs, each festooned with decals of automotive companies whose donations cover most of the costs for the prototypes he builds. All of the cars maintain the same interior and trunk space as the original's. On the outside, the only noticeable but subtle difference is a vertical lengthening that extends the bottom closer to the ground, because they install the batteries underneath the car.

Among their many projects over the years, Frank and his students made a plug-in hybrid in 1997 that could go 60 miles (96 km) on electricity alone and took home the top prize in the Department of Energy's FutureCar Challenge. They replaced a 1996 Ford Taurus's 140-hp, 3,000-cc, 6-cylinder gasoline engine with a tiny 3-cylinder, 660-cc motor, just a quarter the size of the original, combined with a 100-hp electric motor powered by 15kWh of NiMH batteries. The combination gave the plug-in hybrid 140 hp so that it accelerated from 0 to 60 miles (96 km) per hour in 10 seconds, compared with 13 seconds for the original V-6 engine. The system had less than 15% of the moving parts contained in the original.

To cruise at 80 miles (128 km) per hour on highways only requires about 40 hp in an engine, but most cars carry around 250–300 hp. "They're way bigger than you absolutely need," Frank notes. The electric motor provides the performance and acceleration in his plug-in hybrids and the gasoline engine provides the steady-state load for greatest efficiency. With the combined horsepower, "you've got yourself a real high-performance electric car."

The car companies remained resolutely focused on gasoline-only cars, at least in public. The major automakers did their schizoid dance in the late 1990s in which they produced a few electric vehicles and fought to get rid of the clean-air regulations. While they were at it, they suppressed or ignored potential plug-in vehicles.

WHAT MIGHT HAVE BEEN

GM hired Frank to make a plug-in hybrid version of its EV1 that quickly disappeared into the corporate bowels. Chelsea Sexton remembers some GM prototype plug-in hybrids being shown at a few events in the 1990s. The Specialists would describe them to potential customers as an intermediary step between electric vehicles and, in the distance, fuel-cell vehicles. "Every time I explained to somebody what it was, they'd say, 'Oh, yeah, that's exactly what we need.'" But with GM determined to fight off electric-vehicle mandates, it wasn't about to make a case for plug-in hybrids.

The German automaker Mercedes invested heavily in an electric version of its small A-Class city car and planned to launch sales in 1998. But US auto giant Chrysler merged with Mercedes' parent company, Daimler-Benz in 1998 and canceled the program. The car had a real-world driving range of 125 miles (200 km), running on 30kWh of Zebra nickel-sodium-chloride (NaNiCl) batteries that weighed 814 pounds (370 kg) and were installed below the passenger compartment, as in Frank's designs.[6]

Audi tested a plug-in hybrid called the Audi Duo that used diesel instead of gasoline. The Duo reduced emissions because it could run on electricity alone, but when not on electricity, it used more diesel than the comparison car. The company dropped the Duo.[7]

Mitsubishi and Nissan also made progress in developing plug-in hybrids in the early years of the ZEV Mandate, according to

Southern California Edison's Dean Taylor.[8] In 2000 Nissan lobbied the California Air Resources Board to place plug-in hybrids
in the same "gold" category of credits as electric vehicles and hydrogen fuel-cell vehicles, but the Board instead grouped plug-in
hybrids with conventional gasoline-dependent hybrids in its "silver" category. The public never saw a plug-in hybrid from Nissan.

Volkswagen, Fiat, and Renault worked on plug-in hybrids behind the scenes as well. Volvo became the first large car company
to show a plug-in hybrid prototype, displaying the Environmental Concept Car (ECC) in 1992. Based on the Volvo 850 chassis
but built out of aluminum to get the lightest possible weight, the
car ran on a series hybrid system that could recharge its nickel-
cadmium batteries (the best available at the time) by plugging in
or by the gasoline-turbine high-speed generator, which served as
the auxiliary power unit. The ECC could go 53 miles (85 km) on
electricity alone in urban driving. In hybrid mode, it had a fuel
efficiency of 39–45 miles per gallon (5–6 liters per 100 km) for a
total range of 273–315 miles (350–420 km).[9]

The turbine could burn just about anything, giving the ECC
flexibility in the fuel used as backup for electricity. The designers
hoped that the ECC would be "future-proof" by accommodating
a variety of fuels instead of just gasoline, says Ichiro Sugioka,
science officer at the Volvo Monitoring and Concept Center, a
think-tank near Santa Barbara, California.

Plans for plug-in hybrids evolved to the point that Volvo
started producing one called the HEV98 that combined an electric drivetrain with a three-cylinder piston engine. Sugioka drove
an HEV98 during secret testing in Southern California. "I preferred to drive in EV (electric vehicle) mode most of the time. My
commute was about 10 miles each way. So we understand what
this is about," he says.

Volvo started making and testing a fleet of the cars in Sweden,
where the company built all its vehicles, but hadn't officially
launched the product when Ford Motor Company bought Volvo
in 1999 and killed the plug-in hybrid programs. Ford wanted to
maximize its profits and told designers to focus on the company's
core products — SUVs. Engineers also had started designing

plug-in versions of other Volvo vehicles under a secret program code-named Desiree. They took the parallel hybrid drivetrain developed in Desiree and applied it instead to Ford's first hybrid SUV, the Escape hybrid. "Some of us were disappointed, obviously [to see the plug-in hybrids canceled,] but the business decision is, I think, a smart one," Sugioka said.

WHY SUVS?

Among US automakers, SUVs ruled the world not because they were the best vehicles around, but because of government policies that began more than 30 years earlier. President Lyndon Johnson slapped a 25% tax on all imported light trucks in 1964 to retaliate against Europe for restricting imports of frozen chickens from the United States.[10] US automakers exploited that advantage and began advertising their trucks and utility vehicles to all drivers. For decades they fended off government regulations of truck emissions and fuel efficiency by claiming they would hurt farmers, construction workers, and businesses or would force the automakers to lay off workers.[11] Congress exempted light trucks from the 1975 Energy Policy and Conservation Act that set fuel economy standards. The Clean Air Act Amendments of 1977 allowed light trucks to emit two to five times as much pollutants compared with cars. In 1978 Congress exempted light trucks from the tax on gasoline guzzlers and luxury vehicles.

As a result, US car companies could make more profit on trucks, vans, and SUVs compared with passenger cars. They shifted production and marketing strategies toward larger and larger vehicles, spending millions in advertising convincing consumers that this is what they want. By 1977 only one third of light trucks were being used for commercial purposes, the opposite of a decade earlier, *Business Week* magazine reported. In 1998, 47% of vehicles sold in the United States were SUVs and light trucks. By building ever-bigger, heavier trucks and SUVs, the automakers kept pushing them out of vehicle categories covered by updates in federal luxury taxes, the gasoline-guzzler tax, or light-truck fuel-economy standards, and profits remained high even as the vehicles polluted more and wasted more gasoline. Truck sales

Professor Andrew Frank and students converted this Chevrolet Suburban to a plug-in hybrid in 2000–2001, nearly doubling its overall gasoline mileage and giving it a 60-mile range on electricity alone.

accounted for $4 billion of Ford's record $6.5 billion in profits in 1997. The federally controlled Corporate Average Fuel Economy (CAFE) standard for trucks in 1999 was a mere 20.7 miles (33 km) per gallon — the same as it was in 1983.

With SUVs all the rage, Andrew Frank began converting SUVs to show that consumers don't have to give up any size, comfort, or performance to get great mileage and cleaner air with a plug-in hybrid. In 2000 the team acquired the largest SUV, a Chevrolet Suburban, as part of the Future Truck competition and made it a plug-in hybrid, improving its overall gasoline mileage from 15 miles (24 km) per gallon to 29 miles (46 km) per gallon. With a DC brushless electric motor, a second electric motor on the front wheels to give it four-wheel drive, and a 1.9-liter gasoline engine from a Saturn, it weighed 6,000 pounds (2,722 kg) but still could run on electricity alone for 60 miles (96 km) or until its speed passed 60 miles (96 km) per hour, tapping 29kWh of NiMH batteries before relying on gasoline. As a result, the massive plug-in SUV produced fewer emissions than a Honda Insight hybrid car in trips of 87 miles (139 km) or less.

The Electric Power Research Institute's (EPRI's) Bob Graham hired one of Frank's students, Mark Duvall, PhD, and Graham, Duvall, and Southern California Edison's Dean Taylor forged the Hybrid Electric Vehicle Working Group to bring all parties to the table to explore plug-in hybrids. The Working Group released two key studies in 2002 and 2004 showing that plug-in hybrids are feasible and would be cleaner and more efficient than gasoline cars or hybrids and would be accepted by consumers.

In Frank's hands, a 2002 Ford Explorer SUV became a 330-hp plug-in hybrid using a gasoline-sipping 1.9-liter Saturn engine and a 75-kW electric motor for its primary propulsion plus a 60-kW electric drive system for improved handling and efficiency. Even with six college students on board, the plug-in SUV could burn rubber. To keep the weight the same 4,500 pounds (2,041 kg) as the original car, they swapped a few components like the tailgate and seats for lighter versions.

CAR COMPANIES TAKE A LOOK

Frank shipped a converted Mercury Sable plug-in hybrid to Japan in 2003 so that companies doing business with Toyota could take a close look at it. About 250 engineers and executives from two top-level suppliers to Toyota poured over the car.

As a demonstration, Energy Conversion Devices (ECD) bought a 1998 Toyota Prius, put 5kWh of its Ovonic NiMH batteries in it, and made it a plug-in hybrid. ECD replaced the car's battery pack with 20-Ah NiMH batteries to give it triple the power and energy with only a 20% increase in battery pack size. The car could go more than 20 miles (32 km) on electricity alone and get 70–80 miles (112–128 km) per gallon of gasoline.[12] The batteries were not optimized for performance in a plug-in hybrid but worked well even so. (In all of his plug-in hybrid conversions, too, Frank had to make do with NiMH batteries optimized for energy, which were designed for use in electric vehicles, not for plug-in hybrids. Yet his results were impressive.)

Representatives from most of the major auto companies came to see the ECD plug-in Prius. Top engineers from Toyota test drove it, spent more than an hour talking with ECD engineers, and complimented them on their conversion, but Toyota has yet to introduce a plug-in hybrid of its own. ECD employees drove the plug-in Prius until around 2004 and say they don't know where the car is today.

In 2003 AC Propulsion, the small Southern California company whose founders developed the EV1 drivetrain, converted a four-passenger Volkswagen Jetta to a plug-in hybrid that could use either gasoline or natural gas to power the lead-acid batteries supplying the electricity. The car was perhaps the first to demonstrate that electricity could flow two ways — from the grid to the batteries, or from the batteries back to the grid — opening up lots of new possibilities for the benefits of plug-in cars. This led to increasing interest in what came to be known as "vehicle-to-grid" (V2G) connectivity, where plug-in hybrids effectively become part of the utility's power and storage system during the 21 hours per day, on average, that cars are parked.

With funding from the Air Resources Board, EPRI, the South Coast Air Quality Management District, VW, and the National Renewable Energy Laboratory, AC Propulsion showed that the plug-in hybrid Jetta had an all-electric range of 30 miles (48 km), improving efficiency to 27 miles (43 km) per gallon in the city or 34 miles (54 km) per gallon on the highway, compared with the conventional Jetta's 23 and 29 miles (37 and 46km) per gallon, respectively. The plug-in hybrid accelerated faster and could go farther overall — 540 miles (864 km) vs. 435 miles (696 km).

The gasoline served as the backup to the electrical propulsion. The car also could be connected to a natural gas outlet while parked to become a stationary generator, making electricity to feed back into the grid or to power something besides the car. That original conversion was done with lead-acid batteries. The company is replacing those with lithium-polymer batteries under a grant from the South Coast Air Quality Management District, says Tom Gage, head of AC Propulsion.

For the Challenge X competition in 2006, Frank and his students replaced a Chevrolet Equinox SUV engine with electric-power drive and a tiny Toyota Prius gasoline engine modified to run on 85% ethanol and 15% gasoline (a mixture called E85), with a tiny hydrogen fuel cell to power the air conditioning. Their plans include solar panels on a garage or other structure to recharge the batteries and to generate the hydrogen. While a car powered solely by hydrogen doesn't make sense, so little is used in this "flex-fuel" plug-in hybrid for the accessories that it's worth making to show that fossil fuels aren't needed to make small quantities of hydrogen by renewable power, the team believes. Compared with the original Equinox, the plug-in hybrid should accelerate faster, go 40 miles (64 km) on electricity alone, and improve mileage from 19–25 miles (30–38 km) per gallon in the original to 36–39 miles (58–62 km) per gallon in the plug-in hybrid. Its overall range, though, will be shorter — 275 miles (440 km) versus 415 miles (664 km).

Although he's been building prototypes for decades, Frank says that only in the last few years have factors converged to make this the time for plug-in hybrids to come into their own. "There were missing links that really made the concept difficult," he says. One was power electronics to run the electric motors. Insulated gate bipolar transistors (IGBTs) didn't exist until about 10 years ago and weren't high-volume production items until about 5 years ago.

Second was a continuously variable transmission (CVT), in order to get the best fuel efficiency. Though the concept dates back over 100 years to a version made out of leather belts and wooden pulleys, only recently have elegant, durable CVTs been designed for automotive use, including one by Frank that operates with higher efficiency and requires about 12 parts instead of the 700-plus parts in a conventional automatic transmission.

Lastly, improvements in battery technology make plug-in hybrids practical today. In the mid-1990s Frank started using NiMH batteries, which also became the batteries of choice in electric vehicles and hybrids starting in the late 1990s. NiMH batteries provide higher power and energy density with less weight and bulk than previous batteries and have continually surprised everyone with their durability. For his latest project, Frank has moved on to lithium-ion (Li-ion) batteries, which are even lighter but again more powerful and may be on the verge of replacing NiMH in vehicles in the same way that they have taken over the market for powering laptops, cellphones, and other devices.

Frank has been frustrated in his attempts to get others to ask the right questions about plug-in hybrids or to listen to his answers. Rejected by the automotive industry, he became a lone wolf even in academia — "or maybe even worse than that: a twig in a forest," he says — as engineering programs pursued hydrogen fuel-cell vehicles and other topics nearer and dearer to the hearts of their major funders, the car companies.

"Maybe I'm an idealist," says Frank. With the security of his academic position, "I can do what I think needs to be done, and is good for the country, and good for the world." It will take public demand to push politicians to craft the right incentives or penalties that will move the car companies to make plug-in hybrids, he believes. Others will have to help make that happen. He is first and foremost a teacher and a tender of the technology. "I've been promoting this for over 15 years myself but not really getting to the right people. I need help," says Frank, now 72 years old.

Enter Felix Kramer.

A PLUG-IN EPIPHANY

Seeing Frank's plug-in hybrid Explorer at EPRI, and all the excitement about the Prius' EV-mode button, put the fire in Kramer's belly. He would take the concept of plug-in hybrids and market the hell out of it.

For months on end, laboring in his sunny home office amidst chaotic piles and piles of papers, Kramer worked the virtual connections and phone contacts, typing on his laptop computer or standing at his Danish adjustable desk. He knew he needed something that would make the idea real to the average person. Converting one of the hottest cars in America would give him a three-dimensional tool that he could leverage to the max. Until he had a car to show, selling the plug-in hybrid concept was more difficult. "Everyone who met me was cautious because they didn't see it, and they didn't believe I had anything going," he says.

Kramer was in his element, wearing the hats of strategist, organizer, facilitator. He had helped conceptualize, launch, and promote nearly a dozen previous projects and ventures, most of them involving "disruptive" technologies that upended conventional processes and created new mechanisms and markets. "Change is my sweet spot," he said confidently.

Kramer did the CalCars conceptualizing, the planning, the networking, and partnering. In a corporate world he'd be a vice president of marketing and vice president of strategy rolled into one. "I think of myself as doing marketing and public relations, but I try to do it without hype," he says, careful lest anyone think CalCars is peddling vaporware.

What Kramer and Gremban and the CalCars virtual technical group were attempting was, in some ways, harder than Frank's projects. "We can take all the Toyota computers and throw them away, and put our own computer in and program it the way we want to," Frank explained. The PRIUS+ modifications, on the other hand, had to work with what was there already. Batteries had to be found to work within a system that wasn't designed for them. The car's computers, which normally shifted operation away from the hybrid batteries after a shallow discharge, had to be fooled into letting the additional batteries discharge and recharge much more deeply, to provide longer driving in electric mode.

Because of difficulty finding appropriate NiMH batteries, the CalCars team started with inexpensive lead-acid batteries, installed to run in parallel with the Prius' own NiMH batteries and governed by the Toyota battery management system. At first the PRIUS+ could run for only a mile before the battery management computer decided that the battery was depleted, even though it wasn't. Gremban tried hooking it up a different way to the computer's sensors, but after one block of driving, a Fatal Error message appeared and the car stopped running. He had to disconnect the auxiliary battery to get the signal to clear. "We already knew we had to 'lie' to the car, but we didn't know what way was going to work, how to tell the lie," he says.

One of the online discussion group members offered a solution. Greg Hanssen, a former EV1 driver and president of Energy Control Systems Engineering (EnergyCS) of Monrovia, California, could sell CalCars a control/display unit for a couple of thousand dollars to replace and emulate the Toyota battery management system. The Prius computer system is programmed to keep the batteries at least 60% charged. Hanssen would program the new control/display unit to fool the computer into thinking the new batteries were well above 60% state of charge even while the car drained most of their energy, then switch the system back to normal hybrid mode.

EnergyCS was a private company, though, and CalCars aimed to have everything in the PRIUS+ project be open-source so all could share in the knowledge. "We hemmed and hawed a bit because we knew that it would be proprietary," but ultimately went with the EnergyCS controller in order to save time, Gremban said. He since has designed an alternative control/display unit that could be used instead of the EnergyCS unit.

Kramer was pushing to have the car ready by September of 2004, hoping to show it off in Los Angeles at a hearing scheduled by the California Air Resources Board to discuss ways that the state could comply with a pioneering California law restricting greenhouse gas emissions from vehicles. The PRIUS+ wasn't quite ready, but Kramer testified at the CARB hearing anyway. He was offering regulators a way to reduce greenhouse gas emissions, a way to comply with the law, with available technology that fit into the existing infrastructure. The board members listened intently.

He also worked the audience. Kramer had invited Seth Seaberg to the hearing, the head of a southern California company called Clean Tech that converted gasoline cars to run on natural gas. When Kramer introduced Seaberg to Hanssen of EnergyCS, the two businessmen got excited about the commercial possibilities of plug-in hybrids. They began collaborating on their own plug-in Prius conversion, this time using Li-ion batteries.

Kramer also got to meet another key contact whom he'd encouraged to attend the CARB hearing, Danny Hakim, automotive reporter for *The New York Times*. The PRIUS+ story should break first in "the newspaper of record" for maximum exposure, Kramer had decided. He arranged for Hakim to get a ride in an electric Toyota RAV4-EV from Paul Scott, a Southern California electric-vehicle activist who attended the hearing. Kramer offered Hakim first shot at the PRIUS+ story when the car was ready to show.

Gremban and his team got the car running as a plug-in hybrid by November. It still had a few problems, like a ground loop and oscillations. Through e-mails and phone calls with CalCars volunteers, they de-bugged them all. Six months after announcing that they would build a PRIUS+, real-world testing showed that their dream had come true. A mere 10-mile all-electric range on primitive bicycle batteries gave the PRIUS+ an overall fuel efficiency of 100 miles (160 km) per gallon of gasoline, plus electricity, with no loss in performance, even though the extra batteries added 300 pounds (136 kg) to the car.

Later they made plans with a Connecticut company, Electro Energy, to install an NiMH battery pack (instead of lead-acid) into a second Prius. By Gremban's calculations, that would add only 200 pounds (91 kg) to the car and provide a 23-mile (37 km) all-electric range. But that wouldn't happen until 2006. For now, they had the lead-acid PRIUS+, and that was good enough.

PLUG-IN HYBRIDS HIT THE ROAD

With the PRIUS+ running on lead-acid batteries, Kramer worked on bringing different constituencies on board the CalCars train. He talked with entrepreneurs, environmentalists, hydrogen advocates, and public policy analysts. He met with electric-vehicle drivers, pitching plug-in hybrids as the way to introduce Americans to plug-in vehicles. Some were downright hostile. "Maybe 80% of them said, 'Not interested. I want a pure electric vehicle,'" but they were losing their cars as automakers canceled the electric-vehicle programs and reclaimed the leased vehicles, Kramer said. He didn't give up; he went to talk to one Electric Auto Association chapter after another.

To the media, he said as little as possible. A few stealth stories broke anyway in the *Christian Science Monitor* and some small local papers, but for the most part the PRIUS+ was under the media's radar when Kramer and Gremban brought it to Ann Arbor, Michigan, in February 2005 to show it to Hakim.

The *New York Times* story broke in April, the biggest boulder down the mountain in a year-long avalanche of media coverage. On the heels of the *Times, Automotive News, Business Week,* and

Beating the bushes for batteries

One of the first issues the CalCars team faced was the choice of batteries. The Prius used NiMH batteries designed to provide primarily short pulses of high power, known as "power assist" batteries, usually discharging only a shallow amount of the stored electricity per pulse and being recharged by the engine and regenerative braking mechanisms in between pulses. A plug-in hybrid, however, needs a battery that can do this, and handle much deeper discharges and recharges, and also store enough energy to move the car a significant distance without the gasoline engine. The deep-cycle "energy batteries" made for electric vehicles were too much for plug-in hybrids. Instead of the 95-Amp-hour batteries in the Toyota RAV4-EV, or the 6.5-Amp-hour batteries in the Prius, a 25- to 50-Amp-hour battery might be ideal for a plug-in hybrid.

▌ NiMH: Available?

People who called Cobasys, the NiMH battery maker half-owned by ChevronTexaco and ECD in equal shares, were told that the company would not sell small numbers of vehicle batteries to individuals. It would consider only large orders for vehicle batteries — large enough that, coincidentally, only a major automaker could afford to place the order. Others reported conversations with Toyota employees who complained of difficulty in getting NiMH batteries to service the 825 RAV4-EVs that remain in US drivers' hands today. Whenever plug-in hybrid advocates talk about batteries, the question of possible licensing restrictions by Cobasys always comes up.

"Yes, ChevronTexaco is in the business of promoting the NiMH battery, but don't forget who they are," Andrew Frank says. What the company says may not reflect what it does. He obtained the NiMH batteries from ECD for his academic plug-in hybrid projects for $40,000–$100,000 per pack, prices that reflect the experimental nature of his projects, not their cost when mass-produced.

The rumor that Cobasys licensing limited NiMH sales in North America to smaller batteries fits with the fact that the earliest hybrids used D-cell-sized NiMH batteries. Toyota, which now owns 50% of battery-maker Panasonic, has since renegotiated its licensing settlement with Cobasys and used larger NiMH batteries in more recent Prius hybrids. When the Ford Escape hybrid made its debut in 2005, however, inside the hybrid SUV were D-cell-sized batteries. Chevron representatives declined to comment for this book. A Cobasys spokesman said the company would not comment on specific issues out of concern that this book might offend the major automakers that are the company's life blood. "They have in the past been a little bit put off about being preached to about what they should be doing. Our standpoint is, we'll let the market dictate what's going to happen."

Dave Goldstein, president of the Electric Vehicle Association of Washington, DC, dismisses the idea that ChevronTexaco might be limiting access to NiMH batteries for plug-in vehicles as "ridiculous." Goldstein points out that the company has licensed NiMH patents to more than a dozen of the world's leading battery manufacturers, though not for batteries big enough for plug-in hybrids or electric vehicles. The company certainly has the ability to make batteries optimized for plug-in vehicles. One of the batteries that the company displayed at its booth at the Electric Drive Transportation Association conference in December 2005 was a 43-Amp-hour module that might be just about right for a plug-in hybrid. In order to make it worthwhile for a manufacturer to start up a multimillion-dollar assembly line for deep-cycle NiMH batteries, it would have to be guaranteed at least three years of orders of 100,000 or more batteries per year, enough to construct 12,000 EV1 clones, Goldstein estimates. Only a major auto company could afford that, and none of them seem interested. "The batteries will be there. If you build enough vehicles so that the battery companies can build plants instead of experimental lines, they will be there," EPRI's Duvall said in a 2006 radio interview.[13]

Chelsea Sexton has talked with representatives of Cobasys, ECD, and ChevronTexaco about the NiMH issue. Her assessment falls in between the conspiracy theory and those who dismiss it. "Chevron is the one that I have found to be the hindrance," she says. "It does seem that Chevron's the one that's the most resist-ant" to selling batteries for plug-in vehicles.

Chevron representatives have argued that NiMH batteries can't handle a 20-mile electric range in a plug-in hybrid. "Given that the same battery technology has a decade of positive history in electric vehicles, Chevron's current attitude is disconcerting," Sexton says. It also doesn't jibe with real-world evidence. NiMH batteries made by Varta, a Cobasys licensee, performed well enough in the first few plug-in hybrid Sprinter delivery vans in 2005 that DaimlerChrysler and EPRI are expanding the test proj-ect to 40 vans, half with NiMH batteries and half with Li-ion.

Perhaps most telling, Stanford Ovshinsky, the developer of the NiMH battery whose Ovonics company was consumed by ECD and then by Cobasys, said in a June 2006 article that he had de-signed a radical improvement to the batteries that would be per-fect for plug-in cars if only the company would let him proceed.[14]

▌ NiMH: Good enough?

In 2000 battery experts at the US Department of Energy (DOE) decided that NiMH battery technology was so "mature," so proven, safe, and durable, that they could leave any further im-provements to industry, and they moved government research dollars to newer kinds of batteries. By 2003 data from Ford and others showed that NiMH batteries lasted 2,000–3,000 cycles, meaning that a pack should last 130,000–150,000 miles (208,000–240,000 km) in plug-in hybrids or electric vehicles, essentially for the life of the car.[15] In the real world, some five-year-old Toyota RAV4-EVs passed the 100,000-mile mark on their odometers in 2002 on NiMH batteries that were expected to last only 75,000 miles (120,000 km). They've seen no significant degradation in NiMH battery performance or vehicle range, and the vast majority of the batteries reportedly are still running fine in 2006.

As early as 2001, ECD researchers and Frank co-authored a pa-per showing that the company had developed a family of high-power, high-energy NiMH batteries ranging in size from 20 Ah to 90 Ah to meet the needs of a variety of plug-in hybrids. By some estimates, a 4- or 5-kWh NiMH battery would add about 220 pounds (100 kg) to a plug-in hybrid and would allow the car to go 15–20 miles (24–32 km) on electricity alone. Multiple independent tests suggest that NiMH batteries can work well in plug-in hybrids. On the flip side, there is no published data to suggest that they can't do the job.

A Connecticut company, Electro Energy, Inc., claims to have designed a "bipolar" NiMH battery that differs enough from the Cobasys version that it avoids potential patent infringements. The company hoped to start manufacturing them in 2006.

Battery cost is an issue, but even with the cost of the batteries, plug-in cars would be cheaper than conventional cars in the long run because of fuel savings, the 2004 Hybrid Electric Vehicle Working Group study reports. As the escalating production of hybrids brings down the cost of electric-drive motors, motor controllers (inverters), and other electrical hardware, only the barrier of battery costs remain until they too are mass-produced.

The US Advance Battery Consortium, a joint project of car-company and federal representatives, set a goal in the early 1990s of lowering battery costs to $150/kWh. That number hasn't budged since and needs reconsidering because plug-in hybrids can reach cost parity with conventional vehicles even if the batteries cost $380–$471/kWh, the 2004 Hybrid Electric Vehicle Working Group study suggests. It bases that calculation on the expected decrease in costs of components and batteries once they're produced in volume. Component costs should be sufficiently low once automakers produce 100,000 hybrids. The NiMH battery cost will decline to that target if produced in enough volume to make 48,000–150,000 plug-in hybrids each year with 20-mile electric ranges.

Toyota officials insist that the cost of NiMH batteries will remain around $1,100/kWh for the foreseeable future. Even if there's no budge in costs, however, that price applies only to the "power-assist" batteries used in hybrids, Ron Gremban points out, not to less-expensive "power-plus-energy" batteries suited to plug-in hybrids. The cost of NiMH batteries for Prius hybrids fell nearly 40% from the car's introduction in 1997 to 2005, Southern California Edison's Ed Kjaer noted.[16]

▌ Li-ion: Good enough?

While the automakers dithered and stalled any plug-in programs, battery research marched on. NiMH chemistry may (or may not) soon be eclipsed by newer Li-ion batteries, perhaps giving automakers a new reason to stall. Toyota's Dave Hermance used Li-ion as an excuse for not making plug-in hybrids when he told a reporter in April 2006 that Li-ion batteries are necessary and that it will be 10 years before Li-ion batteries are ready.[17]

Li-ion batteries provide 25%–30% more power and energy storage than NiMH and are smaller and lighter. Being newer, they don't have quite the track record of NiMH, and automakers won't use them until there's sufficient data on longevity and cycle life. The beauty of Li-ion is that many different combinations of lithium with other chemistries are possible in batteries, and no one company controls the technology. There should be no bottleneck in the supply of Li-ion batteries, as there may be with NiMH batteries. Some early problems with Li-ion batteries occasionally overheating and causing fires appear to be manageable by the addition of battery-control systems.

In 2000 the DOE turned its attention to Li-ion, and by 2006 one version of Li-ion batteries was deemed to be very good or "mature" — a product being considered by Toyota and by a partnership between the automotive supplier Johnson Controls and battery maker Saft. This Li-ion version may not be optimal for plug-in hybrids in the form tested, but it's a good start, says Tien Duong, team leader in vehicular technology at the DOE.

It may make more sense economically to string together lots of smaller batteries than to produce a smaller number of vehicle-sized batteries, since smaller Li-ion batteries already are widely available for a variety of uses, and larger Li-ion batteries would have fewer applications, he adds. That was the strategy employed by AC Propulsion in making its prototype Tzero sportscar, the one with the 300-mile range.

In order to bring Li-ion battery costs down significantly, automakers would need to commit to producing enough plug-in hybrids so that they comprise 1%–2% of the market eventually, which can take 10–12 years of sales, Duong believes. Gremban says the cost of Li-ion already is comparable with the cost of NiMH batteries, if mass-produced. The price would be around $500–$600/kWh, or around $1,000/kWh in smaller quantities, he estimated.

▌ Other batteries?

Neither NiMH nor Li-ion may be the best choice for plug-in hybrids, however. Sodium-nickel-chloride (NaNiCl) Zebra batteries made by the Swiss firm MES-DEA fall in between NiMH and Li-ion in power and energy characteristics and are available in vehicle-sized versions at less cost. Plug-in hybrids with Zebra batteries are the best option to transition vehicles away from oil, according to a 2005 study by Meridian International Research, an aerospace and alternative energy research firm.[18] Climbing costs for the metals and components in NiMH and Li-ion batteries make them less desireable, Meridian's researchers believe.

Made today in limited volumes, Zebras cost $350–$400/kWh, the price target that the Hybrid Electric Vehicle Working Group said would give plug-in hybrids cost parity with conventional vehicles. In moderate volumes, they would sell for about $220/kWh. The price could fall to $100–$150/kWh with higher production, for the first time meeting the Holy Grail of battery cost set by the USABC in the early 1990s.

The A-Class electric vehicle that Mercedes-Benz had planned to launch in 1998 used primitive Zebra batteries, before being canceled by Chrysler. Modern Zebra batteries in the same car would take it 180 miles (288 km) on one charge, Meridian estimated.[19] Put Zebras in an EV1, and it would approach the distance that automakers insist their customers demand (around 300 miles [480 km]).

Ford designed a similar sodium-sulfur battery chemistry that it tried out in a few dozen Ecostar electric vans starting in the early 1990s. But Ford couldn't work the kinks out of the battery technology and abandoned it in 1994. The batteries needed to be kept at a temperature of 500°F (260°C), and Ford's batteries caught fire.[20]

Today's Zebras also need to be kept hot, and they come packaged in a system that maintains them at a temperature of 662°F

(350°C). "We have evaluated four generations of these batteries in the national labs," says the DOE's Duong. "It's very safe. It's funny — it's very hot, but it's very safe," and may be a good choice for plug-in vehicles.

Ron Gremban rejected Zebra batteries for the PRIUS+ and is skeptical about their suitability for plug-in hybrids. There were Zebra units that were the right size and voltage but with only a quarter of the power output needed for the PRIUS+. "The power output may be enough, however, for full EVs, with their larger battery packs," he adds.

▋ CalCars picks nickel

Gremban picked NiMH for the second PRIUS+ (after the first one with lead-acid batteries) because the automakers already use them in hybrids. "They clearly don't have an excuse that this is a chemistry that is not going to work, or that it's unsafe, or has problems. They're already using it. All they can say is that these particular NiMH batteries have not been tested" specifically for plug-in hybrids, he says. The PRIUS+, he adds with a smile, "is a confrontational project."

Whichever batteries the automakers choose for plug-in hybrids, "The technology is viable. We are very excited about it. No doubt about it — it's doable," says the DOE's Duong. "We strongly believe in plug-in hybrid applications."

In the big picture, here's the catch: Better batteries always are in development. Incremental improvements constantly are being made to established batteries. When should a car company jump in and commit to a particular battery chemistry? When is good, good enough? Clearly, well-functioning and affordable plug-in hybrids could be made with today's batteries, but there will have to be other forces besides battery readiness to induce an automaker to take the plunge.

others ran stories on plug-in hybrids. *Newsweek* magazine columnist Fareed Zakaria described the possibility of cars that got 500 miles (800 km) per gallon of gasoline if a plug-in hybrid had a flexible-fuel tank that ran on 85% ethanol and 15% gasoline (known as E85).

Within days, blogs and discussion groups were all over the PRIUS+ — Slashdot, Engadget, Autoblog, and PriusChat. EVWorld.com built a website dedicated to plug-in hybrids. People debated what to call this new kind of car. Electric hybrids? Pluggable hybrid electric vehicles? Gasoline-optional hybrid electric vehicles? Flex-fuel hybrids? TV and radio came calling, including a National Public Radio "Science Friday" program on plug-in hybrids for Earth Day.

By now Greg Hanssen of EnergyCS was driving his own bright-blue plug-in Prius prototype in Southern California. Running on 180 pounds (82 kg) of Li-ion batteries, it was getting 120–180 miles (192–288 km) per gallon in city driving. After the first 50–60 miles (80–96 km), the gasoline efficiency reverts to the Prius's normal 40–50 miles (64–80 km) per gallon. EnergyCS shipped the car to Monaco in the spring of 2005 to show to engineers from Renault and other European automotive companies at EVS21, the international business convention for the electric-vehicle industry. They entered the car in the annual Tour del Sol fuel economy rally in Saratoga, NY, and won their class by averaging 102 miles (163 km) per gallon over a 150-mile (240-km) course. The night before the race, they filled up the car with $1 worth of electricity and $4 worth of gasoline.

In May 2005 EnergyCS and Clean Tech announced a new company — EDrive Systems of Monrovia, California — with hopes of offering consumers a plug-in Prius conversion service in the future for a fee of $10,000–$12,000 per car.

The South Coast Air Quality Management District pledged $130,000 that month for three plug-in hybrid projects: EnergyCS would make a plug-in Prius for testing; AC Propulsion would upgrade its VW Jetta plug-in hybrid to further demonstrate vehicle-to-grid charging possibilities, and the rest of the funds would support a joint project by EPRI and DaimlerChrysler to demonstrate the plug-in hybrid Dodge Sprinter delivery van. That same month, Kramer and Gremban began online discussions to convert the Ford Escape hybrid into a plug-in SUV. Down the line, they could see conversions of Hyundai or Nissan hybrids and Toyota's Lexus and Highlander hybrids.

The starting gun had fired. Plug-in hybrids were off and running.

Kramer began wheeling and dealing to establish a company that could partner with a major automaker and become a qualified vehicle modifier (QVM), converting shells of the company's hybrid vehicles into plug-in hybrids with its blessing. Ford, for example, gives its blessing to 14 QVMs that turn its vehicles into stretch limousines, hearses, specialty vans, and other modifications. Becoming a QVM would be a way to meet demand for the first 10,000–100,000 plug-in hybrids that Kramer figured it will take before an automaker is convinced there's a real market for them. He began talking with Andrew Frank and others to set up a supply chain of components, so the parts would be there when needed.

"This is all very ambitious, but we think it's possible," says Kramer. Eventually, a car company would want to make the plug-in hybrids itself and probably would put Kramer's QVM out of business. "Then we do the whole thing over again, but next time not for a conversion, but for a fully optimized new vehicle designed from the ground up as a plug-in hybrid."

CalCars and EnergyCS estimate that a plug-in hybrid would sell for $3,000 more than a hybrid or $5,000 more than a non-hybrid car if mass-produced by a major automaker, and will save drivers money over the life of the car.

To the media, the car companies kept repeating their mantra that NiMH batteries aren't acceptable, and that Li-ion batteries aren't ready to be put in cars that they'd have to warrantee. "You never know, we may be looking at another EV1-like battery electric vehicle that would be featured in lithium ion," GM spokesman Dave Barthmuss said in February 2006. "I'm not really sure the electric vehicle is dead. I think it is being fine-tuned and researched."

Simply put, the major automakers didn't market a plug-in hybrid because they didn't want to and they didn't have to. The weakening of the ZEV Mandate delayed the introduction of plug-in hybrids and let the automakers take functioning zero-emission electric cars off the road. But the electric cars that they were rounding up for crushing weren't dead yet.

THE STREET ACTIVISTS

CHAPTER 5

Acting Up for Plug-ins

MARC GELLER BUZZED the intercom for the narrow beige-and-brick building and waited. Blue and red tiles on the sidewalk offset the dreariness of adjacent gum-spotted pavers. Even the drug dealers on the corner didn't look so bad in the bright San Francisco sunlight, next to a man selling carnations and roses from a five-gallon bucket in front of the Cash-a-Check doorway.

This was the Mission District, ground zero for some of the most innovative non-profit organizations and scrappiest political activists in the world. Geller felt right at home. He rode the slow, noisy elevator to the second floor and walked down the narrow hallway, past Environmentalists Against the War and into the sky-lit office of Global Exchange.

It was the kind of room he'd come to know since the age of 16 when he walked into the Manhattan office of Mobilization Against the War in Vietnam — rooms full of posters and leaflets and socialist workers subtly competing to see who's more radical. The Indian-print bedspreads covering the lobby chairs on the beat-up wooden floor were timeless. A five-foot-tall peace sign built from metal rifle parts hung on the wall surrounded by giant, colorful papier-mâché sculptures of a dragonfly, butterflies, and a flying frog. Art was everywhere.

Jason Mark, Global Exchange coordinator for the Jumpstart Ford campaign, greeted Geller and ushered him into a fishbowl of a room off the main conference area. Geller squeezed his lanky body into one of the four worn-out office chairs crowding the square aquamarine Formica table, below a poster for fair-trade coffee. Mark closed the door.

Geller was grateful for the audience, and frustrated. He had tried to recruit larger environmental organizations to help save the electric cars that were being crushed by the automakers. He'd hounded journalists and politicians, too. One by one they'd blown him off. Geller wasn't asking for the world — he knew that zero-emission electric vehicles weren't *the* answer to auto pollution and oil addiction. Better fuel efficiency of gasoline cars would be needed, too, but it shouldn't be the only tactic on the agenda. It would have been fine if he could have gotten environmentalists or journalists to at least include electric vehicles in the broader package of solutions, but Geller couldn't get even that. He hadn't been to a gasoline station in three years of driving the Th!nk; he knew that car companies could offer zero-emission options. That's all he was asking — to give consumers the option of electric cars.

Driving by the Ford dealer one day, Geller had seen activists holding a huge banner of the Statue of Liberty in a gas mask. "Declare Independence from Oil — Demand Zero-Emission Cars," it read. That's how he learned that Global Exchange and the Rainforest Action Network had started the Jumpstart Ford campaign.

In 2003, the 100-year anniversary of its founding, Ford had the worst record of any major automaker in terms of fuel efficiency and, thus, greenhouse gas emissions. Its average fleet fuel efficiency, driven down by the huge trucks and SUVs that Ford favors, was 18.8 miles (30 km) per gallon, worse than the Model T's. Ford liked to advertise itself as a green car company, but the facts spoke otherwise.

Now Ford was ending the lease on Geller's electric Th!nk City car and reclaiming all the Th!nks and electric Ranger trucks that it had built before demolition of California's Zero-Emission Vehicle (ZEV) Mandate. Ford originally told Th!nk drivers that it would return the cars to its subsidiary in Norway, which had supplied the cars under a temporary waiver from the US Department of Transportation as a "demonstration project." Because the Th!nks had not been crash-tested to US specifications, they couldn't remain on the road here, now that Ford had canceled its electric-car program. But instead of shipping the cars back to Norway, where waiting lists of people hoped to buy one, Ford began scrapping the Th!nks.

Mark spread some of the Jumpstart Ford literature before Geller to show him their demands: Ford vehicles that get 50 miles (80 km) per gallon by 2010, and zero-emission vehicles by 2020. Geller planted a forefinger on the brochure. "I drove here in a zero-emission vehicle built by Ford! You're calling for it 16 years from now. There's a disconnect here. They're taking away the car that you're calling for 16 years from now, and I want to keep it," he said forcefully.

"Until you demand that which they've already proven they can do, and to the extent that you continue to talk just about gasoline mileage, you've made the car companies very happy, because they know how to kill any legislative attempts at better CAFE standards," Geller said, referring to Corporate Average Fuel Economy regulations.

"You can meet with the auto executives every year — even all the CEOs — but as long as you're still talking only about gasoline, it means nothing really has to change. When you leave the room, I believe they pull out a bottle of expensive Scotch and say, 'Cheers,' to each other, because they know they can go on with business as usual," Geller said. "You think of yourselves as a radical organization? Frankly, it's…it's…retarded, for lack of a better word, for a radical organization not to be calling for a cleaner alternative that already exists."

At age 29, Mark had never owned a car, and he hoped to avoid buying one for as long as he could. He'd never met someone so passionate about a car. But he — and Global Exchange — understood the need for a variety of solutions to America's destructive oil addiction. It would take CAFE standards, and biofuels, and hybrids, and more mass transit, and high-speed bullet trains, and bicycling, smart community planning, and more.

The materials he'd developed for the Jumpstart Ford campaign hadn't included plug-in vehicles. Not because he didn't agree with them; he just hadn't known about them. Mark spent his first few years with Global Exchange doing international human rights work. He'd been neck-deep in campaigns against Nike and Gap sweatshops during all the ZEV Mandate battles. Still, it's not like he wasn't paying attention. If anything, he was hyper-informed. He read two printed newspapers per day and several more online and constantly listened to National Public Radio and other programs like a true news junky. The fact that he didn't know about electric cars says something about how the issue fell out of the public eye. Reassigned to create the new Jumpstart Ford campaign, he spent a month just reading up on the science of peak oil and climate change, and still didn't learn about electric vehicles.

But now Mark got it. Surely there was a way, he agreed with Geller, that Jumpstart Ford could incorporate the Th!nk issue, and maybe help save the cars at the same time.

Driving his little red Th!nk home for dinner with his housemates in the Haight-Ashbury, Geller was ecstatic. Finally! In 2003 he had helped organize a demonstration at the local Ford dealer when the company canceled the Th!nk program, but it hadn't received much attention. The Ford employees had been sympathetic and even threw them a barbecue during the event. The media hardly noticed. Now, with Jumpstart Ford's resources behind them, maybe they could really make some noise.

It never ceased to amaze Geller how much he loved this car. He certainly hadn't expected to. For 20 years he'd driven old Citroen wagons, which were weird looking and a hassle but the most comfortable cars in the world. Sure, Citroen parts were hard to find, since they stopped making the cars in 1975, and the cars left a trail of hydraulic fluid wherever they went. He knew that this was environmentally irresponsible, but what the hell, he thought, cars pollute. When his last Citroen was dying in 2000 and none of the used cars he saw seemed half as interesting, he started to look at the electric cars he'd heard something about. He began reading online and came in contact with the community of electric car drivers. The difficulty he encountered getting an electric car only increased his desire for one.

Geller test drove an EV1, but the Saturn dealer told him he'd never get one. He called the Honda dealer about the EV Plus, but was told that he was too late — had he called six months earlier, maybe he could have leased one, but they weren't going to offer any more. He took the old Citroen on one last road trip to Sacramento to test drive an electric Ranger, but he didn't really want a truck.

In May of 2001, he found the Th!nk. He had to call and call the dealer to get a lease, but finally he was driving a tiny, candy-red two-seater hatchback made with a tubular aluminum frame and a dent-resistant, recyclable thermoplastic body; barely bigger than a golf cart. "It was much less car than I ever wanted," especially after his two-ton French marvels that were big enough to sleep in. To his surprise, "the car worked so well, and met my needs. It just presented to me revelation after revelation."

Never having to use gasoline and oil made him realize how much had been going into — and coming out of — his old cars. The Th!nk had a 35-mile range (50 if you really nursed the accelerator), but that was fine 95% of the time. There were lots of people around who were willing to swap their gasoline cars with him if he wanted to make a longer trip. And best of all, because the car was less than 10 feet long, parking was a breeze in a city with notoriously difficult street parking.

Then al Qaeda attacked the United States on September 11. To Geller, the connection with oil was plain: We buy their oil, enriching anti-democratic regimes that in turn finance radical Islam, then we have to pay again to fight them. His little Th!nk symbolized a solution that Geller felt should be available to all Americans who were pissed off at the terrorists: a way to drive without oil; a way to stick it to the oil companies, too. And not cause pollution. All of which inspired Geller to install solar panels on the house — the solar shtetl on Haight, he called it.

The electric plug so demeaned by the automakers suddenly seemed to him not a tether to inconvenience, but a door to freedom.

When Ford scratched the Th!nk program in 2003, GM EV1s already were being confiscated and sent to the crusher. Geller couldn't understand why no one was out protesting all this. He was late to the electric-vehicle scene, though, and many of the earlier activists were burned out after losing the ZEV Mandate battle. Most of them weren't naturally inclined to demonstrate anyway. They were engineers and techies, for the most part; they wrote letters, and hired lawyers. On top of that, the organization that normally speaks up for plug-in vehicles — the national Electric Auto Association — was sidetracked by an internal, organizational crisis, and hadn't fully recovered.

For Geller it was second nature to publicly protest a wrong, whether or not it produces immediate results. He took to the streets with other students at Grinnell College in rural Iowa in 1976 after a CIA-backed coup toppled the legitimately elected Socialist government of Salvador Allende in Chile. As a photographer for the gay press in the 1980s and 1990s, he'd shot plenty of Act Up protests and Queer Nation demonstrations and seen their power in getting attention paid by the media and the government to their issues. Those demonstrations produced practical results in the form of better and more widely available AIDS medications.

If he had to let go of his Th!nk, he would do it loudly.

When Geller got home, he called Norway to talk to Rune Haaland, whom he had met on the Th!nk listserv, and told him of his talk with Jason Mark at Global Exchange. The Norwegians weren't taking the loss of the Th!nk quietly, either. Haaland knew that a Norwegian company, Elbil Norge, had offered to buy the cars back from Ford, and the Norwegian Transport Minister had written to Ford on their behalf. Norwegians loved the Th!nks and considered them a symbol of the country's innovation and environmentalism. But Ford never responded.

Haaland called Truls Gulowsen of Greenpeace in Norway to fill him in on the situation. Gulowsen hooked up with Kristen Caspar of Greenpeace USA at one of the groups' organizing conferences in the Netherlands. Late one night at an Amsterdam bar, Gulowsen and Caspar crowded into a bathroom together, shut the door, and placed a cellphone call to the United States.

Jennifer Krill answered on the other end. Krill was to Rainforest Action Network (RAN) what Jason Mark was to Global Exchange: the brains and energy behind Jumpstart Ford. Caspar and Gulowsen started telling her all about this important campaign that they should run together to save the electric cars and show how the car companies were undermining serious efforts to reduce oil dependency and greenhouse gases.

"What are you talking about?" Krill asked. "You're Greenpeace. What do you need us for?" Because, they explained, the focus was on Ford.

INTERNATIONAL OUTCRY

At 5:40 A.M. on a sunny August 24, 2004, two Greenpeace activists entered Ford headquarters in Oslo, Norway, and climbed the stairs to the roof. As they unfurled a large banner reading "Ford: Don't Crush Th!nk," 10 more activists on the ground got ready to hand informational flyers to arriving employees, who hadn't been informed by the company that the Th!nks were being scrapped. The action hit the morning news before Ford executives were out of bed.

A sympathy demonstration by 20 electric-vehicle drivers joined the media outside the Ford building. Greenpeace repeated how Elbil Norge was offering Ford $1 million for the 360 Th!nks that had been shipped to the United States, and how Ford had snubbed the transport minister. After 13 hours, the Norwegian Ford managing director came out to tell the protesters that the company's head of European sales and the vice president for European communications would meet with them the day after tomorrow. Greenpeace accepted the offer, took down the banner, and went home.

With an eight-hour time difference between Norway and San Francisco, stories already were moving on the wires and CNN when Geller, Mark, Krill, and 50 other activists converged on the Ford dealership that day. A quiet funeral procession of 10 electric vehicles escorted Geller's Th!nk and another that were to be returned to Ford that day. They parked the two Th!nks at the dealer entrance and covered them with American flags for the ceremony, surrounded by signs and banners supporting the demonstration. Veiled and genuinely tearful mourners paid their respects, decrying the loss of gasoline-free, zero-emission vehicles at the same time that US soldiers were dying in Iraq. Blood for oil.

A black-robed and hooded "Death" played taps on a bugle as members of Veterans for Peace ceremoniously folded the flags into neat triangles and presented them to the Th!nk drivers. With a big sigh, Geller went inside and handed over his keys. He would never forget this day. It was his 50th birthday.

Two days later, the Ford officials met with Greenpeace Norway activists who gave the company a three-week deadline to "Th!nk twice" about destroying the electric cars. The Ford executives also met with the transport minister and at a joint press conference afterward said that the company would re-evaluate its management of the Th!nks. As the press conference was in progress, an independent group of activists in western Norway smashed a gasoline car outside a Ford dealership.

Jumpstart Ford and Greenpeace worked their media contacts over the next three weeks, keeping the story in play. Nick Carter in Santa Rosa, California, and other Th!nk drivers staged more funerals as they were forced to return their cars. Two other Norwegian companies offered to buy the Th!nks from Ford, and droves of Norwegians signed up on waiting lists, hoping to get one of the cars.

Ford's Director of Environmental Strategies, Niel Golightly, told the press that a third of the US Th!nks already had been crushed.[1] "Clearly, the entire industry could build nothing but zero-emission cars today if we wanted to," but carmakers weren't convinced that people want them, he said.[2] Selling 10,000 electric cars per year would make the endeavor economically feasible, another Ford spokesperson estimated.[3]

One day after the activists' deadline, Ford announced that it would meet the activists' main demand — to send the remaining

Dave Raboy at the 2005 vigil to save his electric Ranger truck from being destroyed by Ford.

Th!nks back to drivers in Norway. In the end, Ford agreed to do simply what it had said it would do in the first place. In the very end, it didn't even do that, instead "processing" only 160 Th!nks for reuse, crushing the rest or keeping some for parts.[4]

The victory was more than symbolic to electric-vehicle activists; it was galvanizing. Since Ford had agreed not to destroy the Th!nks, why not the electric Ranger trucks? Why not keep those on the roads — US roads?

Geller hooked up Jumpstart Ford with Ranger drivers who had been resisting returning two of the trucks at the end of their leases, and they planned a vigil at a dealership in the California capital, Sacramento. Solar installer William Korthoff brought his Ranger up from Southern California. The campaign caught media interest largely because of the other Ranger owners — ranchers David Raboy and Heather Bernikoff-Raboy of Catheys Valley.

With cowboy hats, a truck, and solar panels on their ranch for the house and truck, the Raboys were as American as apple pie. As American as Ford. They were demanding that Ford sell the electric Ranger trucks, including ones already reclaimed from other leaseholders, restart production of electric vehicles, and dramatically improve efficiency and reduce greenhouse gas emissions throughout Ford's fleet.

Ford had leased about 200 Rangers to individuals and 1,500 to commercial fleets. By this time, only around a dozen were in private hands and 180 in fleets, but others were in Ford's control, awaiting their fate. The company said it was pulling the trucks out of service because batteries were not available.[5] The earlier Rangers had used lead-acid batteries, but the more recent ones used nickel-metal hydride (NiMH) batteries.

On a foggy, bone-chilling day in January of 2005, they held a press conference with the trucks outside the Sacramento dealer, and settled in to wait. Not knowing how long they could sustain it but determined to stay as long as they could, they kept vigil, giving media interviews from a rocking chair in the back of Korthoff's Ranger. Geller and other sympathizers bundled up in winter clothing, came to Sacramento, and kept them company when they could, or stayed informed through Jumpstart Ford and Raboy's own website, DontCrush.com. Felix Kramer showed up in the PRIUS+ and introduced them to a plug-in hybrid. They used the bathroom in the casino across the street, powered their laptops from a solar panel trailered there by a supporter, and counted unsold SUVs on the Ford lot when they got really bored. Electric-vehicle activists and Jumpstart Ford participants all over the state peppered Ford and the media with calls and letters.

Eight days later, Ford capitulated. Not only would it stop destroying the Rangers, but it would sell the trucks for $1 each to current leaseholders. Ex-leaseholders could enter a lottery to buy the remaining trucks for about $6,000 each. But the company would not restart production of electric vehicles or improve emissions from its gasoline vehicles.

Saving the Rangers floored even old-guard electric-vehicle enthusiasts who'd criticized the Th!nk demonstration as unseemly and likely to do more harm than good. These were tangible results — keeping the vehicles on the road.

And if the Fords could be saved, why not what remained of the other electric vehicles?

It was too late for the 300 or so Honda EV+s. Honda had been one of the earliest to round up its electric vehicles, and for a while no one outside the company knew their fate; not until, that is, a viewer recognized the car on a 2004 episode of the PBS television show, "California's Green:"

Show host: We're going to be able to see cars shredded today. That's not something that most of us get to see.
Shredder: We shred about a car a minute. A thousand cars a day on a good day.
Host: What's interesting is the first thing we noticed when we drove up here — you're going to be shredding some new cars here too. [They walk up to a Honda EV+.] These look like perfectly good cars. Why are you shredding them up?
Shredder: It's a little bit of a mystery, really. Since I've been here the last eight years, they bring us these cars from the dealerships, and they say that they're test cars, and they've been brought over to test various emissions, and the insurance companies won't reinsure them, so they have to watch them destroyed here.
Host: That seems like a shame. It's terrible. I'd like to drive off with one of these things...

If the Hondas couldn't be saved, what about the 1,300 Toyota RAV4-EVs? Or the 490 Chevrolet S10 pickups? Or Nissan's Hyperminis and Sentras that never made it into private hands but were leased only to fleets?

Through the Ford actions, electric-vehicle activists in Northern and Southern California had built relationships and were inspired to work together again. They named their alliance DontCrush.com: The Campaign To Save Electric Cars and set up regular conference calls to discuss their next move. Should they go after GM or Toyota? When someone spotted a GM lot in Burbank, California, with 78 EV1s, DontCrush.com members were surprised and excited. Everyone thought the EV1 was extinct. Apparently, it wasn't dead yet.

THE LAST STAND

Chelsea Sexton sat in her sleeping bag in her car at 3 A.M., blogging to the world. It was day 27 of the EV1 Vigil. She was alone on the street of this residential Burbank neighborhood, outside the wide brick building and fenced lot of EV1s at the GM Training Center, just down the road from Disney Studios.

DontCrush.com and its allied organizations had held a press conference on the front lawn of the facility on February 16, 2005, and then simply didn't leave. A half-dozen key organizers and various supporters took turns keeping up a round-the-clock presence and held weekend rallies and press conferences. They recruited 78 people to make written commitments to purchase the EV1s for the residual value stated in the lease — nearly $25,000 each — and to sign waivers releasing GM from parts, service, warranty, or liability commitments.

GM ignored their $2 million offer to save the EV1s, which didn't surprise Sexton but irked her anyway. GM already had received up to $13,000 in public taxpayers' money for each EV1 plus $18,000 in lease payments. The $25,000 per car that vigilers were offering would bring GM's potential take to $56,000 for a car that cost about $44,000. What other GM vehicle commanded a $12,000 premium, especially after it was at least three years old?

The vigil hadn't been easy; the days were long, and the nights were desolate and boring, not to mention cold and uncomfortable. Nearly non-stop rains, wind, and flooding replaced the normally mild Southern California weather that year, literally blowing the vigil away. During the day a handful of vigilers would huddle under a canopy on the sidewalk, calling or e-mailing the media and supporters, trying to keep their electronic equipment dry.

Two weeks into the vigil, while trying to catch some sleep in a supporter's RAV4-EV, Sexton spent most of the night comforting a volunteer from Rainforest Action Network who was there with her. A fierce storm raged outside, and every time the wind shook the SUV, she freaked. Suddenly they saw the canopy blow over, the metal poles bent and tossed about by the wind. They jumped out into the storm and wrestled it all out of the street, to keep it from blowing into cars. Once they'd tied it down, Sexton leaned over the swift-flowing water in the gutter and hacked up a huge hunk of phlegm. She knew instinctively that she'd developed pneumonia during the weeks on the vigil, but she hadn't seen a doctor yet. The diagnosis would come later; she didn't want to be kept away from the protest.

It was overwhelming to wonder how long they could stick this out. Instead they focused on the next immediate, small task. How could they get one more person involved? One more news article? One more statement of support?

Little things kept their spirits up. Surprise pizza deliveries, courtesy of Ron Freund in Northern California and Dave Goldstein in Washington, DC. Late-night e-mails with encouraging words from all over the country. A solar array to power the coffee maker. Visits at odd hours from people they'd only met online. And the larger community that turned out for the Saturday rallies. But they missed their families and the normal rhythms of life.

GM's response to the media was to repeat refrains heard from all the car companies. They had to take the electric vehicles off the road because if they developed problems in the future, it would hurt their brand image, they said. Plus, there wouldn't be enough parts to service the vehicles, since they were being discontinued. (No other discontinued car in history was destroyed instead of sold to waiting customers.) And the electric-vehicle "enthusiasts," God bless 'em, just weren't enough to make a market.

One of the GM executives slipped, though, and mentioned the waiting list. The secret was out. At last Sexton could talk about it — 5,000 people had wanted EV1s, and many others couldn't even get on the list. GM then said the company had contacted everyone on the waiting list and only 50 people remained interested in leasing an EV1. Multiple people on the list said they never heard from GM. The company's only response to the activists' offer for the cars so far was to send a transport truck on day 17 and haul away six of the EV1s. They followed the truck in Sexton's black, two-door Saturn coupe. (Despite everything, "I'm still a Saturn/GM kind of girl," she says.) In Palm Springs, they called ahead to supporters in Arizona to pick up the chase and turned around to head back to the vigil. Heading out of Palm Springs, Sexton spoke with a GM spokesman by cellphone. She didn't envy GM's public relations staff, who had to defend the company in this situation, so she was unflaggingly polite.

"I respect what you all have been doing. I wish people like you worked here," GM's Dave Barthmuss told her. Sexton couldn't help but smile. "I did work for you guys, Dave. If you think about it, I'm still just doing the very same thing General Motors hired me to do nine years ago — promote the EV1."

At the vigil site, even in the smallest moments when the streets were dark and quiet and the GM guards had gone home, she couldn't help but feel a part of something big. Something so compelling that she didn't have to ask herself whether or not to keep at it; because this wasn't just about the car. Sexton was more realistic than any of them about the unlikelihood of GM releasing the EV1s. No, this was about giving Americans a choice to drive clean cars and, through that choice, to have cleaner air, less global-warming emissions, and greater national security through independence from oil. The EV1 was a symbol of what's possible.

Three weeks into the vigil, actor and biodiesel activist Woody Harrelson's website brought support from a broad new group of people. Media interest picked up, fascinated by the fact that they were still there. On day 27, Sexton saw three black, ominously familiar semitrailer trucks pull into the GM lot. These were the only kind of trucks that had transported EV1s when the program was alive, and there could be no question why they were here now. Sexton, Paul Scott, and other key organizers frantically phoned supporters to get to the site as quickly as they could.

The trucks loaded up 21 EV1s, but before they could leave, actresses Alexandra Paul and Colette Divine blocked the driveway in Paul's RAV4-EV. They locked their doors when police were called in and faced down the trucks for two hours, finally surrendering when police threatened to smash the windows. Police arrested them for civil disobedience, moved the SUV, and the trucks rumbled away, but national media ran the story.

Sexton and two other vigilers followed the trucks in her Saturn. One of the truckers smiled and waved at them as they crossed the state line, knowing that the Arizona Highway Patrol officers he had called were waiting to stop Sexton's car. The troopers pulled Sexton over for making the trucker feel "harassed and in fear for his life." They lectured her for an hour about what can happen to a girl like her on back roads by truckers who feel threatened, and then let her go without a citation.

The three activists drove through the night back to Burbank just in time to see nine more auto transport trucks arrive, plus a lot of police officers. GM employees loaded the EV1s in a rush, tires squealing and body panels cracking against each other, trying to get the trucks on their way before the vigilers could attract the kind of press coverage they'd had the day before. This time, each truck had a police escort, but no one followed the trucks. Everyone knew where they were going — to GM's desert "proving grounds," to join the stacks of other crushed EV1s.

Two weeks after the end of the vigil, Sexton received a form letter sent by GM's former EV1 Brand Manager Ken Stewart to anyone who had offered to buy one of the EV1s in the Burbank lot. This was the man who had told Sexton that "if there's demand, we'll build you more cars," and inspired her to help start the EV1 waiting list. In the letter, Stewart said he was writing to correct the "misconception" that there had ever been a waiting list. GM would stick to its line that EV1 production stopped because there wasn't enough demand.

THE ALLIED AND THE ABSENT

In the battles to save the Th!nks, Rangers, and EV1s, a number of non-profits and environmental groups stepped to the plate. Global Exchange, Rainforest Action Network, Greenpeace, and DontCrush.com did the heavy lifting but drew support from the American Lung Association, Earth Resource Foundation, the Coalition for Clean Air, Environment Now, Global Green, Energy Independence Now, and the Electric Auto Association.

Other voices that could have been effective in publicly championing zero-emission vehicles were missing in action — some of the major environmental organizations. Instead, their ambivalent or inaccurate stances left open the question: Are plug-in cars really green?

CHAPTER 6

Where Were the Greens?

T HE US HAS 4% of the world's population but contributes 22% of man-made greenhouse gases to Earth's atmosphere. One third of US greenhouse gas emissions comes out of cars and light trucks; another third comes out of power plants. To avoid climate catastrophe, we must clean up both the cars and the power plants.

Greenhouse gases like carbon dioxide (CO_2) trap the sun's heat around the planet. Thanks to humans, more CO_2 is in the atmosphere today than at any point during the last 650,000 years.[1] Since we started burning fossil fuels in the Industrial Revolution, atmospheric CO_2 has climbed 35%. The 10 warmest years since the time of the Vikings all happened since the mid-1990s, and 2005 was the hottest year on record. On average, the world is one degree warmer than usual, but the polar areas are warming twice as fast as elsewhere. More than 20% of the polar ice cap has melted since 1979. Glaciers are melting, polar bears are drowning, sea levels are rising, and increases in air and water temperatures are creating more killer hurricanes and other extreme weather events around the globe. If we don't reduce carbon pollution, we're likely to reach a tipping point that could plunge Europe into another ice age, desiccate Africa in droughts, and disrupt ecosystems around the world.

US carbon emissions are expected to increase 37% by 2030.[2] Climate scientists suggest that just to stabilize greenhouse gas concentrations in the atmosphere we need to reduce today's levels of greenhouse gas emissions by 55%–85%, to below 2.5 tons (2.3 metric tons) per person per year. In car terms, for every SUV producing 20 tons (18 metric tons) of CO_2 per year, we'd need 18 people producing less than 1 ton (0.9 metric ton) of CO_2 per year.[3]

Vehicles that rely on gasoline — hybrid or non-hybrid — can't get us to below 1 ton of CO_2 per year, per car. Plug-in hybrids and electric vehicles can. Multiple studies show that these vehicles reduce greenhouse gas emissions compared with conventional cars or hybrids, even when factoring in both tailpipe emissions and the "upstream" emissions produced when making gas or electricity. (See "The plug versus the pump," elsewhere in this chapter.)

So why aren't the largest environmental organizations — the Sierra Club, the Natural Resources Defense Council (NRDC), and the Union of Concerned Scientists (UCS) — leading the charge for plug-in vehicles? These groups have long and strong histories of trying to shut down polluting power plants, clean up coal-plant pollution in the Midwest, stop mountaintop removal to mine for coal, and fight the hazards of nuclear power. Just as any group pushing for cleaner cars has experienced the lies and dirty tactics of the auto industry, so too anyone battling for cleaner power knows to be skeptical about what the power companies say.

It's counter-intuitive to many environmentalists to accept the idea that powering cars on electricity — a strategy endorsed by the electrical utilities — could reduce greenhouse gas emissions. And yet it's true. The NRDC and the UCS did a gut-check on that by analyzing the emissions benefits of electric vehicles in the 1990s. Satisfied with the results, they became advocates for California's Zero-Emission Vehicle (ZEV) Mandate.

In a 1994 study, the UCS calculated that electric vehicles in Los Angeles would cut carbon emissions by 71% compared with an ultra-low-emission gasoline vehicle, even after accounting for

Emissions Alphabet Soup

- **CO_2** — Carbon dioxide, the main greenhouse gas that comes out of vehicles and fossil-fueled power plants, contributing to global warming.
- **CO** — Carbon monoxide. Inhaled, it blocks transport of oxygen to the brain, heart, and vital organs.
- **NOx** — Nitrogen oxides, which irritate lungs, increase risk of respiratory infections, and help create other respiratory irritants like ground-level ozone and particulate matter.
- **PM** — Particulate matter, which may penetrate deep into lungs and cause asthma and other respiratory illnesses.
- **SOx** — Sulfur oxides can react in the atmosphere to form fine particles that pose respiratory risks.
- **VOC** or **ROG** — Volatile organic compounds, which help create harmful ground-level ozone; also called reactive organic gases.

power plant emissions created in making the electricity for the vehicles. Other pollutants would decrease too: 99% less carbon monoxide (CO) and volatile organic compounds (VOC); 60%–64% less nitrous oxides (NOx), and 56% less particulate matter (PM). Sulfur oxide (SOx) production would increase by 17%,[4] but existing regulations already are reducing NOx and SOx emissions from power plants, and that trend will continue.

"We're very confident and very aggressive in stating that electric vehicles can provide a 70% reduction in greenhouse gases and over 90% reduction in criteria air pollutants in California and the Northeast. We're less aggressive in talking about the Midwest because of the power mix," which includes more coal, says Jason Mark, director of the clean vehicles program for the UCS.

A 1994 report by the NRDC and the Environmental Defense Fund cited a California Air Resources Board (CARB) study showing that after taking power plants into account, electric vehicles in Los Angeles still would reduce CO_2 emissions by 50%, CO by 99%, and NOx by 89% compared with gasoline cars.[5] More recent calculations based on the mixture of power sources in the US electrical grid (which is about 50% dirty coal) found similar results. Plug-in cars reduce greenhouse gases because they clean up the worst offender, the tailpipe.

Even the most recent analyses that compare plug-in hybrids or electric vehicles with the best hybrids (the cleanest gasoline cars) show that both kinds of plug-in vehicles produce less overall CO_2 than gasoline-dependent hybrids. It's time to end the myth that plug-in vehicles aren't clean.

Just as automakers' attacks on electric vehicles and their promises of hydrogen fuel-cell cars wore down California regulators, they wore down environmentalists. By the 2003 CARB hearings, testimony by NRDC and UCS representatives focused on trying to get regulators to increase the number of hydrogen fuel-cell cars required in that year's revision of the ZEV Mandate.

"At that time, the orientation of the Air Resources Board was so focused on fuel cells that we were putting it in those terms," said Jason Mark of the UCS.

Besides looking toward hydrogen, the big enviros' clean-car campaigns fell back on advocating for greater fuel efficiency, and added hybrids to the mix. Attempts to raise Corporate Average Fuel Economy (CAFE) standards or improve vehicle efficiency focused on getting automakers to install variable valve timing, six-speed transmissions, hybrid powertrains, and other technology that can make vehicles use less gasoline, and so produce less CO_2. The technology exists for car companies to make all vehicles average 40 miles (64 km) per gallon within 10 years, which would save 4 million barrels of oil per day.

Unfortunately, attempts to increase CAFE standards have been stymied for decades. Auto industry lobbyists, claiming that higher standards would ruin their companies and force them to lay off workers, always have managed to convince enough legislators to avoid any significant change in fuel-efficiency standards.

Most of the enviros' clean-car campaigns also see their role as educating consumers to pick the greenest cars that are available from large car companies and encouraging automakers to build more of them. Toyota developed a cozy relationship with environmental groups because of its Prius hybrid, even as it was crushing its zero-emission RAV4-EVs behind the scenes. The Sierra Club went so far as agreeing in 2005 to promote Ford's Mercury Mariner Hybrid SUV to its 300,000 members. Ford planned to build only 2,000 of them in 2006, expanding to 4,000 per year eventually. The Sierra Club chose the Mariner not because it's the most fuel-efficient vehicle around but because at 31 miles (50 km) per gallon it's more efficient than Ford's other gasoline-guzzlers and because it promotes hybrid technology.

GREENWASHING AHEAD

Introducing a greener technology doesn't guarantee that it will be used for environmental benefit. This certainly was the case with hybrids. While the first Toyota and Honda hybrids improved gasoline mileage by 40%–50% compared with their gasoline counterparts, automakers quickly started using the electric drive system to add power to vehicles instead of better gasoline mileage. Honda's first hybrid Accord got a mere 16% better fuel efficiency than a conventional four-cylinder Accord, and in 2006 its hybrid and non-hybrid Accords didn't differ from each other at all in gasoline mileage.

Estimated mileage ratings went downhill with each new hybrid introduced in the first nine years of hybrids as manufacturers shifted the emphasis from efficiency to size and power: Honda Insight, 60mpg; Toyota Prius, 52mpg; Honda Civic, 48mpg; Ford Escape SUV, 30mpg; Honda Accord, 32mpg; GM Sierra truck, 19mpg; and Chevrolet Silverado truck, 18mpg. The hybrid Silverado and Sierra trucks gain only 10% in fuel efficiency — the equivalent of 1–2 miles (2–3 km) more per gallon — over their conventional counterparts, but they offer electrical outlets under the rear seat where power tools or other devices can be plugged in to the hybrid's batteries. Since these, the slide in hybrid fuel efficiency has been partially reversed, but newer models still only get 26–40mpg.

Plug-in hybrid technology, in comparison, can be applied to all vehicle platforms and will make a measurable difference with each. Even a plug-in hybrid Hummer could be a zero-emission vehicle on short trips within its electric range, though that's hardly the best use of plug-in technology. Automakers could squander the benefits of plug-in hybrids by designing them to emphasize power over efficiency, if allowed.

There's no guarantee that people who buy plug-in hybrids will plug them in. If that happens, however, nothing is lost environmentally, because the vehicles still would operate like hybrids, the cleanest cars available today. Consumers know how to recognize a good deal, though: plugging in at night will save them money and require fewer trips to the gasoline station. Most of them will plug in.

USING OFF-PEAK POWER

Some environmentalists worry that introducing plug-in hybrids will force us to build lots more polluting power plants, but that scenario just doesn't add up. Wally Rippel, an engineer with AeroVironment, calculated that if all 200 million cars in America were electric, they'd use about 20% of the electricity being generated today. Plug-in hybrids would use far less.

That doesn't mean we'd need to build 20% more power plants, though. Plug-in cars get recharged mainly at night, when many plants either waste the energy they produce or power down without shutting off completely, because there's less demand than during the day. This "excess capacity" at night (the amount of power that *could* be generated) was enough in 2000 to accommodate more than 43 million electric vehicles, the US Department of Energy estimated.[6] Since plug-in hybrids would recharge with a quarter or a half of the amount of electricity needed by electric vehicles, we wouldn't need any new power plants until well over 80 million of them are on the road.

Those kinds of numbers don't happen overnight. Seven years after hybrids were introduced to the US market, sales barely topped 500,000 in mid-2006. Even if automakers introduce plug-in hybrids now, it will take a long time before there are tens of millions of them — which is all the more reason to start making them sooner rather than later. During that time, the electrical grid will be getting cleaner, because current laws require it. Regulations capping carbon emissions are needed and are likely to be adopted within a few years. Plug-in vehicles already make environmental sense, and once carbon caps on power plants are in place, they'll be even cleaner.

FLIRTING WITH PLUG-INS

Some of the major environmental groups are warming up to plug-in hybrids, but large organizations don't turn on a dime, and sometimes their left hand doesn't know what the right hand is doing.

A 2003 UCS report rated plug-in hybrids highest of any hybrids for their potential to improve energy security and to reduce harm to the environment.[7] The UCS in 2006 launched <www.hybridcenter.org> to help consumers differentiate between "full" hybrids and "hollow" ones, and pointed to plug-in hybrids as the most efficient option. At the same time, contradicting its own studies, the UCS repeated the smokestacks myth in a Q&A section of its HybridCenter website: "Using dirty sources of electricity to recharge a plug-in can cause just as many, or more, problems than plugging in solves," it stated. There is no evidence to support that.

The NRDC echoed that fiction in a 2006 press release: "While plug-in hybrids could play a role in reducing our transportation oil demand, using our electricity grid to power vehicles could simply shift emissions of global warming pollution from tailpipes to electric power plants unless strong emission limits are in place."

Roland Hwang, NRDC's vehicles policy director, says that he thinks plug-in hybrids should reduce greenhouse gases compared with a conventional car, but that the group wants to conduct its own study to be sure. "It's just that I've lived through the battery electric and hydrogen enthusiasm waves, so I've advised my folks internally that we must do our homework, thoroughly understand the technology and the environmental impacts, before getting more involved in advocating for any one particular technology," he says.

Recent NRDC studies moved the group away from the hydrogen hype[8] and gave them a scientific basis for supporting

The Plug Versus the Pump

To reduce global-warming gases, plug-in hybrids are a winner according to my overview[9] of more than 30 studies, analyses, and presentations on well-to-wheels emissions from plug-in hybrids or electric vehicles. No matter where the electricity comes from, plug-in hybrids reduce CO_2 emissions by 37%–77% compared with conventional gasoline cars and by 19%–54% compared with hybrids.

Similarly, electric vehicles reduce overall CO_2 emissions by 11%–100% compared with conventional gasoline cars or by 24%–54% compared with hybrids if the electricity comes from a mix of power sources. If the electricity comes strictly from coal, however, electric vehicles may increase CO_2 30%–49% compared with hybrids, but compared with conventional cars they would reduce CO_2 by 0%–59%. If the electricity comes from wind or solar power, electric vehicles eliminate all greenhouse gases and other emissions. Electricity from natural gas produces emission levels between those of coal and renewable energy sources.

Hybrids make up only about 1% of the US light-vehicle fleet so far, so electric vehicles produce less greenhouse gases than 99% of vehicles on the road today, even using solely coal-fired electricity. Only 11 US states (most of them sparsely populated) get more than 80% of their electricity from coal. It makes no sense to say that electric vehicles shouldn't be sold anywhere because of these states. Californians alone buy 10% of US vehicles. Both electric vehicles and plug-in hybrids will reduce greenhouse gas emissions in the US as a whole, and plug-in hybrids will do so even in states with 100% coal power.

▌ Assessing the data

Why is there such a spread in the numbers for estimated emission reductions? Will plug-in hybrids reduce CO_2 emissions by 37% or by 77%? Do electric vehicles reduce CO_2 emissions by 11% or by 100%?

Results vary depending on what is being studied, where, and how. It's important to compare apples with apples. For instance,

Toyota spokespeople have claimed that an electric vehicle produces more greenhouse gases than a Toyota Prius hybrid, but they compared the smaller, lighter Prius sedan with the bulkier, less aerodynamic RAV4-EV SUV, which is not a fair comparison. Compare well-to-wheels emissions from a Prius and a plug-in Prius, and the regular Prius loses. Compare well-to-wheels emissions from a RAV4 and a RAV4-EV, and the electric RAV4 is cleaner.

The number of studies and the consistency of their findings matter in assessing results.

- All 21 comparisons of plug-in hybrids with regular hybrids found that plug-in hybrids create less overall CO_2.
- Of the nine analyses comparing electric vehicles with hybrids, seven said the electrics would decrease CO_2. The other two were the only analyses to assume 100% coal-powered electricity, and they found less CO_2 with the hybrids. The small number of studies in this category (both pro and con) leaves all their findings questionable, but the trend favors electric vehicles over hybrids, especially with the current mix of power plants.
- Many more studies compared plug-in hybrids or electric vehicles with conventional gasoline cars than with hybrids. All but one said gasoline cars create more overall CO_2. The one anomaly was an informal analysis meant to generate discussion, its author said. It assumed electricity came strictly from coal and suggested that electric vehicles and gasoline cars would produce the same amounts of CO_2. In comparison, five other analyses also assumed the power came strictly from coal, and they found that electric vehicles would reduce CO_2 by 17%–59%.

The sophistication of a study also makes a difference. For these complex calculations, the widely recognized gold standard is the Greenhouse Gases, Regulated Emissions, and Energy Use in Transportation (GREET) computer modeling created by Argonne National Laboratory. The Lab's Michael Q. Wang, PhD, says he prefers to use an "average" mix of US power sources for countrywide comparisons of vehicles, and he rejects the more speculative "marginal mix" used by some other emissions studies. His approach is the more conservative one.

In his 2001 GREET 1.6 analysis of vehicles and fuels (the most recent), both plug-in hybrids and electric vehicles generate significantly less CO_2, CO, and VOCs compared with hybrids using reformulated gasoline. Plug-in hybrids produce about the same levels of NOx and PM as hybrids, but more SOx. Electric vehicles produce more NOx, SOx, and PM than hybrids.[11] (But the NOx and SOx won't necessarily be released into the atmosphere; see "Beyond CO_2," below.) Wang now is using the new GREET 1.7 model to conduct a more detailed study of plug-in hybrids. Results won't be ready for years.

▌ Beyond CO_2

The purported downside of electric vehicles and plug-in hybrids, regarding emissions, is a 17%–296% increased production of SOx or SO_2. The data are split on NOx and PM — these might increase, decrease, or be equivalent, depending on the study.

Regulations are in place and technology exists to contain these "extra" emissions, says Charles Garlow of the US Environmental Protection Agency's Air Enforcement Division. Scrubbers can handle SOx and mercury, and baghouses and electrostatic precipitators can contain PM. The 1990 acid-rain amendments to the Clean Air Act cap total acid-rain emissions, so no matter how much electricity we generate, total SOx and acid-rain emissions will be declining if the Act is enforced. Scrubbers also can contain mercury, and they work best to contain mercury if used in combination with the selective catalytic reduction technology used to scrub out NOx. While there is no absolute cap on PM emissions, federal rules are in place to ensure that these emissions will decrease as well.

Indeed, between 1993 and 2004, as US utilities increased electricity production to feed an energy-hungry society, CO_2 emissions increased from 2.2 billion to 2.7 billion tons per year (from 2 billion to 2.4 billion metric tons). During that same timespan, however, SOx emissions declined from 16.5 million to 11.4 million tons per year (from 15 million to 10 million metric tons), and NOx emissions fell by half, from 8.8 million to 4.4 million tons per year (from 8 million to 4 million metric tons), despite the increase in electricity.[12]

Cleaning up a few thousand centralized power plants is simpler than trying to control emissions from 200 million cars,
trucks, and SUVs, whose emissions concentrate where the most
people live, and whose engines get dirtier as they age. In contrast,
electricity keeps getting cleaner as we replace aging inefficient
plants with newer technology and with zero-emission renewable
energy.

*For a more detailed description of the studies on emissions, see my
Web site at <www.sherryboschert.com/FAQ.html>.*

bio-fuels.[10] The NRDC has begun a detailed study of well-to-
wheels emissions for plug-in hybrids, in conjunction with the
Electric Power Research Institute (EPRI) and energy expert
Joseph Romm. Results are expected in late 2006 or early 2007.

RUNNING ON RENEWABLES

The years required for plug-in hybrids to grow in number will
provide time to tap more clean, renewable power, such as solar
and wind energy. Better yet, plug-in hybrids will help make renewable power more prevalent and more affordable.

That's why Austin Energy, the publicly owned utility of
Austin, Texas, began plug-in hybrid promotion campaigns in
2005. Austin uses more renewable power than any US city, most
of it wind power. In Texas and elsewhere, a lot of wind power goes
to waste because it blows at night, when few customers need it
and there's no place to store it. With plug-in hybrids charging at
night, that wind power can be stored in batteries. City officials
voted to set aside $1 million to give consumers incentives to pur-
chase plug-in hybrids when they become available, and began
lobbying other US cities to promote plug-in hybrids too.

"We're going to replace Middle East oil with west Texas
wind," says Austin Energy's Roger Duncan.

Harnessing even 20% of the world's wind energy would
produce eight times more electricity than humans consumed
around the globe in 2000, scientists at Stanford University calculated in 2005.[13] The US Department of Energy in 1991 reported
that three states — Kansas, North Dakota, and Texas — could

produce enough wind energy to meet US demand for electricity, and advances in technology since then more than double the amount of power that could be harvested, environmentalist Lester R. Brown noted.[14]

Plug-in hybrid technology "gives autos access to America's vast, largely untapped, wind resources," wrote Brown, founder of the Worldwatch Institute and president of the Earth Policy Institute. Wind technology and companies already exist. With the right incentives, it would be relatively easy to increase US wind-generating capacity 10-fold. "Within a matter of years, thousands of ranchers or farmers could be earning far more from electricity sales than from agriculture," he notes, and the two industries could exist side by side.

Plug-in hybrids bring many of the same advantages in partnership with solar power or other renewables like wave energy, tidal energy, or hydroelectric power. I'm not talking about putting solar panels on a car. That wouldn't be worth the expense and the weight added to the car. Today, it's much more efficient to put panels on a home, building, or carport to feed electricity to the grid and bring it back out again to the plug-in hybrid. As solar photovoltaic technology evolves, integrating lightweight solar cells into the bodies of vehicles could make a significant contribution. If 5 million plug-in hybrids each had 200 Watts of photovoltaic capacity built into them, the total power generated would be similar to that of a large electrical plant.[15]

If all the solar power falling on the United States could be converted to electricity, it would produce about 10 times as much electricity as we consume.[16] By some estimates, using available rooftop space for solar panels could provide 710,000 megaWatts of electricity, close to the country's current capacity of 950,000 megaWatts. Put another way, panels on a 100-mile-by-100-mile piece of land (10,000 square miles, or 25,600 square km) could produce enough electricity to meet US electrical needs, provided there's someplace to store what's not used immediately. Panels on an area the same size as what's being used for US military bases (30 million acres) could generate power equivalent to the US annual electricity *and* fuels consumption.[17]

Solar panels become more cost-effective if the power replaces not just $0.10/kWh electricity from the grid, but $2.50 gasoline at the pump. The investment in the panels gets paid back much quicker when combined with a plug-in hybrid. If the power flows two ways — from the grid to the vehicle and back again — we've got the financial underpinnings of a much more sustainable society.

GIVE AND TAKE: VEHICLE TO GRID

The average car gets driven 3 hours a day; the other 21 hours it could be plugged in, sopping up wind or solar energy for storage, and ready to feed power back into the grid if needed when thousands of people turn on their air conditioners on a hot summer afternoon. Utilities and consumers would sign "vehicle-to-grid" (or V2G) contracts, bringing flexibility to the grid for the utility and extra income for the driver. Computer monitoring could make sure the car's batteries are recharged when the driver gets back to it, or the car could simply drive in hybrid mode.

Japanese designers envisioned something like this when they built the Toyota Dream House, on display in that country in 2005, that included solar panels on the roof and sides of the home. The garage contains a neighborhood electric vehicle and a plug-in Prius hybrid, which can be used to supply electricity for 36 hours in an emergency, such as an earthquake that causes a blackout.

This is hardly pie-in-the-sky fantasy. Toyota is testing V2G linkage in a Prius with a rural electric cooperative in Oklahoma, Toyota's Cindy Knight said. AC Propulsion demonstrated V2G in a converted Volkswagen Beetle in 2002 and a VW Jetta conversion in 2003. The company estimated in 2001 that 1 million V2G vehicles could generate electricity equivalent to that produced by 20 average-sized power plants. Each V2G vehicle might earn its owner as much as $3,000 per year.

An analysis by academics at Vermont's Green Mountain College determined that the economics of V2G make sense for both utilities and drivers. With each vehicle providing power with a net value of over $2,000 annually, that's "enough to quickly and economically usher in the era of a low- and zero-pollution light-vehicle fleet," they wrote in 2002.[18]

Other academics at the University of Delaware calculated some of the synergies between vehicle and grid power. Solar power peaks at noon, but the highest demands for electricity come several hours later. If 26% (23 million) of the US light-vehicle fleet consisted of electric RAV4-EVs with V2G capability, the vehicles would store enough solar energy to handle that peak load, even if only half the vehicles were plugged in when the grid needed to take some of their power back. For large-scale use of wind power, the grid will need more sources of "regulation" power (used to keep the frequency and voltage steady for a few minutes at a time, many times a day). If half of US electricity generation came from wind, we'd only need 3% of cars, SUVs, and light trucks (fewer than 6 million) to be electric vehicles with V2G contracts to regulate the grid, assuming half the vehicles are available at any one time.[19] US Department of Energy studies suggest that widespread implementation of V2G technology could increase usage of wind power by a factor of three, the DOE's Philip Patterson says.

Northern California-based Pacific Gas & Electric teamed with EPRI to start testing in the summer of 2006 a plug-in hybrid version of a "trouble truck," one of the large trucks with bucket lifts to raise workers up to damaged lines. The utility expects the plug-in hybrid to improve fuel economy by 30%–50%, reduce emissions by 50%–70%, and allow 6–8 hours of stationary operation without idling (reducing the exhaust workers breathe). It will act as a standby generator providing 25–30kW of power in an emergency, and because it will be plugged in at night, recharging aligns with renewable energy. "Wind energy in our area tends to happen in the wee hours of the morning," PG&E's Brian Stokes, manager of its cleaner transportation group, said at a December 2005 meeting of the Electric Drive Transportation Association. Wide use of cars and trucks with vehicle-to-grid technology could generate enough power to reduce the need for central power generation capacity by 20% by the year 2050, EPRI estimated.[20]

BIOFUELS AS BACKUP

The simplest plug-in hybrids can get 100 miles (160 km) per gallon of gasoline, but they might get 500–1,000 miles (800–1,600 km) per gallon of gasoline if the primary fuel that backs up the electric drive is not gasoline but mainly a biofuel, such as ethanol or biodiesel, with a little gasoline mixed in for easier ignition in cold weather. Today most ethanol comes from food crops like corn or sugar cane, and most biodiesel comes from soy beans or palm oil, none of which are ideal for long-term sustainability, but these can help us shift away from oil initially. Other, more sustainable sources of biofuels have attracted the greatest interest — namely, biomass. Outside a turkey processing plant in Carthage, Missouri, animal waste is turned into biodiesel, for example.

Cellulosic ethanol made from perennial grasses and plant waste like corn stalks, among other things, could replace about half of current transportation petroleum in 40 years while cutting vehicle greenhouse gas emissions by more than 80%, the Natural Resources Defense Council concluded in its 2004 report, "Growing Energy." That time frame could be shortened greatly if we use plug-in hybrids, which reduce the need for ethanol. The world's first large-scale cellulosic ethanol plants planned to open in 2006 in European countries. There are not enough refueling stations to get any kind of biofuels to most US drivers today. Biofuel boosters and plug-in hybrid proponents, however, are beginning to come together to form a power alliance that will help us get off petroleum and reduce greenhouse gas emissions faster than with either technology alone.

All of these strategies — plug-in hybrids, biofuels, renewable power, vehicle-to-grid connectivity — will help us rapidly move away from fossil fuels. That will reduce our greenhouse gas emissions, help clean up pollutants, and save consumers money in the long run. Compared with oil, electricity is cleaner, cheaper, and domestic.

It's that "domestic" advantage that has caught the interest of a powerful constituency. In the past two years, they've assertively aligned themselves in support of plug-in hybrids: the neoconservative national security hawks.

THE NATIONAL SECURITY HAWKS

CHAPTER 7

Jim Woolsey Gets Wired

"I HAVE SOME BAD NEWS," US Secretary of Homeland Security R. James Woolsey[1] announced. Things were about to go from bad to worse.

The eight other presidential cabinet secretaries and advisors seated around the horseshoe table immediately stopped talking. They already were dealing with a crisis — two terrorist attacks in Saudi Arabia on June 23, 2005,[2] including machine-gun fire and explosions at a natural gas facility and the hijacking of an oil supertanker near an eastern Saudi port. The President had convened this executive committee of top federal officials to discuss response options and advise him on strategy. They were to report back to him in a few hours.

Now what?

Woolsey tersely relayed a report from his deputy: An oil tanker entering the Port of Valdez, Alaska, rammed another tanker in an apparent terrorist attack. A massive oil spill ignited a fire that was spreading throughout the harbor. At least 12 of the 18 oil-holding tanks in Valdez were burning. The Coast Guard was reporting gunfire at the tank farm and requesting emergency air evacuation for burn victims. Guard commanders believe two teams of terrorists were involved — one on board the ship that entered the Port and another near the storage tanks.

First Saudi Arabia, now Alaska. "Multiple attacks on two continents certainly sounds like Al Qaeda," National Security Advisor Robert M. Gates said grimly. "We have to assume that further attacks can be coming."

In Saudi Arabia, security forces had thwarted the tanker hijacking, but the sabotage at the natural gas plant shut down operations there. Normally the gas gets used domestically, and now the Saudis would have to divert 250,000 barrels per day of oil intended for export to cover domestic needs, putting a significant dent in the oil supplies for other countries. Even worse, though, was the significance of the event. The Saudis supply 10% of the world's oil, around 9 million barrels a day. If that source is not safe, neither is the global economy, which relies heavily on oil.

The Port of Valdez normally ships about 1 million barrels of oil a day from Alaska, mainly to US West Coast destinations. How would the US economy function without it? Secretary of Energy Linda Stuntz summed it up for her colleagues: "We're going to have to accelerate our efforts to reduce the role of oil in our economy" and look at ways of getting more oil from non-OPEC countries in the interim.

Only six months before, in December of 2004, this same committee — the secretaries of state, defense, treasury, energy, the interior, and homeland security, plus the national economic advisor, the national security advisor, and the chairman of the joint chiefs of staff — had met to formulate advice for the President about civil unrest in Nigeria, the fifth-biggest source of oil sales to the United States. Foreign oil companies had fled Nigeria to avoid the violence, closing some oil wells and cutting oil production by 600,000 barrels a day. Bad timing, too — the Nigerian problem coincided with an extended cold snap in Northern Hemisphere weather that added demand for another 700,000 barrels of oil per day for heating.

All in all, the world needed close to 88 million barrels a day at that point, but only about 85.6 million could be pumped out of the ground, which meant at least a three-month shortfall that

R. James Woolsey.

spiked oil prices and fueled economic insecurity. Saudi Arabia had demanded political concessions in exchange for ramping up oil production within five to six months to ease the Nigerian crisis. To his credit, the President stood firm and rejected political bargaining, even though it meant that consumers paid $1 more for a gallon of gasoline at the pump.

Woolsey recalled that during that premonition of today's more severe crises, some of his colleagues just didn't seem to get it. Secretary of State Richard N. Haass had downplayed the situation. "Maybe I'm missing something here, but I don't quite see the crisis," he had said. "Let's make sure we agree that we've actually got something other than an economic bump in the road here rather than something that's a full-fledged foreign policy or national security crisis" before taking any drastic action.

It reminded Woolsey of all the terrorism "experts" before September 11, 2001, who said that terrorism was just a nuisance, not a major long-term problem. As a former director of the Central Intelligence Agency, that kind of talk drove him crazy. Terrorism was real, and it wasn't going away. Now it should be clear that US energy supplies were insecure and that the energy problem would not go away.

Woolsey urged the committee then to put a long-term strategy in place immediately. "We've got to get beyond just dealing with crises. We've got to deal with this on a much more fundamental basis," he said. Nigeria was the least of it. When asked to compensate for the Nigerian shortfall in oil production, the Saudis had listed several conditions: The United States would back off on pressure for democratic reform and elections, drop investigations of money being laundered in Saudi Arabia for Al Qaeda, and turn full attention to resolving the Arab-Israeli conflict.

"We're just getting started here. The next Saudi demands are going to be much more extreme than this. They already have spent $80 billion to $90 billion over the course of the last 25 years spreading Wahhabi beliefs around the world — fanatically anti-Shiite and anti-Suffi Muslims, anti-Jewish, anti-Christian, anti-female, anti-democracy, anti-modernity," he said. "This business of our backing off on democracy and human rights and not criticizing them — that's just the first installment."

The committee argued the pros and cons of easing the Nigerian shortfall by tapping the strategic petroleum reserve, a 684-million-barrel "bank" of oil kept for use in a US emergency. The chairman of the Joint Chiefs of Staff, General P. X. Kelley, advised leaving the reserve alone. With other serious threats on the horizon — tensions with Iran and North Korea — the military might need every drop of oil in the reserve if a conflict arose.

Woolsey agreed. "One trick in this business is using a crisis as an opportunity to make some long-term changes that need to get made," he reiterated. "I don't think we should move quickly" to deplete the reserves. "Things could get a lot worse than this."

And now they had.

CRIPPLING THE ECONOMY

The Alaska and Saudi attacks knocked more than twice as much oil out of world supplies as the Nigerian unrest had six months earlier. Overall, the world now was facing a shortfall of close to 3 million barrels per day. It would take at least six months for the Valdez facilities to get back to normal operations.

A video in which Osama bin Laden had talked about attacking the American economy burned in Woolsey's memory like a hot poker.

Secretary of the Treasury Don Nickles called in a staff energy expert to forecast the economic fallout from the attacks. Although the United States is the third-largest oil producer — after Russia and Saudi Arabia — it's also the largest oil consumer, chugging 25% of world oil production. Transportation sucks up about half of all oil in the Unites States. Without oil, US vehicles would come to a halt, because 97% of US transportation requires oil.

Because most people, businesses, and governments that rely on oil can't immediately reduce their use of it, any major interruption sends oil and gasoline prices skyrocketing and devastates business as usual. The US had learned that lesson in 1973–1974 when the Arab-controlled Organization of Petroleum Exporting Countries (OPEC) slapped an embargo on oil sales to the United States in retaliation for US support of Israel in the Arab-Israeli war. The price of gasoline nearly quadrupled, the stock market tanked, and President Nixon called for voluntary rationing of gasoline. That crisis led to approval of the trans-Alaska pipeline and prompted creation of the strategic petroleum reserve. In real dollars, a gallon of gasoline today is cheaper than it was in the 1970s. A barrel of oil that might sell for $58 in 2005 would have fetched $80 in 1980 currency.

Today's loss of Alaskan and Saudi oil was likely to shoot prices to over $120 per barrel, the treasury secretary's aide explained. US drivers and homeowners would soon be looking at prices higher than $5 per gallon of gasoline or heating oil. The average driver would pay an extra $3,500 a year for gasoline, and homes heated with oil would need an extra $2,400 a year to stay warm, if driving and heating habits remained unchanged. Those would be huge hits to the median household income of $43,000.

"This could be a devastating winter for people on fixed incomes, for poorer Americans," not to mention the hardships that would be faced by people in the poorer nations of the world who could ill afford zooming energy prices, National Economic Advisor Gene Sperling said.

Consumer confidence would likely plummet. Inflation would spike to over 12% and settle at around 5.5%, considerably higher than before the attacks. Some 850,000 jobs would be lost as companies struggled to handle the high oil prices. Auto companies, airlines, and the hotel and travel industry would be hit especially hard. If oil prices stayed that high for a year, economic growth would stall and the country would enter a recession. Another 2.3 million jobs would be lost next year. The stock market would take a dive, and the US trade deficit would balloon by millions of dollars.

The United States is accustomed to borrowing about $800 billion per year from other countries — including many of the oil-producing states — that stockpile US dollars and lend them back to us. About $250 billion year, or $1 billion every workday, of that is used to import oil. This arrangement has allowed the United States to spend more money than it takes in, and to import more goods than it exports. If the oil crises made foreign governments unwilling to accumulate dollars, or if they decided to start selling dollars, the value of the dollar would fall sharply. Interest rates would rise. The US budget — already running a deficit and financially stretched — would have to be cut drastically.

The whole situation could feed on itself to get even worse, the aide added. During the initial steep climb in oil prices, producers would rush to get oil to market to cash in, because they would expect prices to drop. But as the price continues to climb, what economists call "contagion" could set in, where the futures markets expect oil prices to go up, motivating oil brokers to hold some oil off the market in hope of selling it for a higher price later. Decisive, pre-emptive action should be considered to avoid this damaging market psychology, the aide suggested.

Sperling was the first to say what was on most committee members' minds: "If there ever was a time" to use the strategic petroleum reserve, the national economic advisor said, "this is it." Releasing 2 million barrels a day for at least 60 days, with a review after 30 days, would be a dramatic, calming response and would only deplete the reserve by about 20%, he said.

Secretary of State Richard N. Haas chimed in: "If the strategic petroleum reserve was not created for circumstances like this, then I don't really understand why we bothered to create it."

Woolsey disagreed. "It's not that I'm opposed to taking decisive action. It's that I don't think releasing a few more barrels from the strategic petroleum reserve is decisive action." He tried again to open his colleagues' eyes to the true nature of the problem.

"The problem is that we are at war with a fanatical enemy that has lots of patience and wants to destroy not only our infrastructure, but us. We are not in uncharted waters; we have been in major wars before. It's just that the weapons have been different. We were not dealing with religious fanatics who were willing to wait 2, 3, 4, 5, 6 years or the rest of their lives in order to strike a body blow at our economy and our survival."

As Woolsey saw it, the United States is fighting World War IV — the war against terrorism (with the Cold War being World War III). He feared that World War IV could last considerably longer than either World War I or II. He only hoped it wouldn't match the four-plus decades of the Cold War.

At the root of much of the anti-Western terrorism was the Wahhabi doctrine advocated by a fundamentalist Sunni Muslim sect. The dominant faith in Saudi Arabia for more than two centuries, Wahhabism is a severe form of Islam mandating a literal interpretation of the Koran and condemning anyone who doesn't practice this form of Islam as a heathen and an enemy.

In the past 30 years, the Saudis have spent an estimated $70 billion to $100 billion spreading Wahhabi beliefs by funding schools and mosques throughout the world. Some oil-rich families have directly funded terrorist groups that claim to carry out the duties of Wahhabism. Osama bin Laden, whose views on underlying issues are essentially the same as Wahhabism, has called for major reductions in oil production and advocated oil prices of $200 per barrel or more in order to cripple his industrialized enemies.

Woolsey used this analogy: Wahhabism is to terrorism as German nationalism was to the Nazis. Not all angry German nationalists became Nazis, and not all Wahhabi believers become terrorists, but in each case the broader doctrine of hatred nurtured a totalitarian movement.

Because the United States is dependent on oil, and 45% of oil comes just from Saudi Arabia, Iran, and Iraq, we're paying for both sides of the war — ours and the terrorists', Woolsey reasoned. How could he get his colleagues to see the bigger picture and respond accordingly?

ACTION IN WARTIME

Woolsey liked to describe himself as an old-fashioned, Scoop Jackson-style Democrat (conservative in foreign affairs but more liberal on domestic issues). His hawkish, unwavering stance in support of President Bush's invasion of Iraq had flustered some members of his own party and earned him the respect of some Republicans. He held open the option of US military action elsewhere in the Middle East too — in Iran, for instance.

Perhaps his service as CIA director under President Clinton, his current seat on the National Commission on Energy Policy, and other experiences allowed him to see the current oil crises as part of a whole in ways that the other executive committee members couldn't, he thought. "We should start from the position that we're at war. We need to figure out how to fight that war effectively, not how to moderate in the short-run some admittedly unfortunate and painful economic conditions that various parts of our economy are in," he explained. "We've got to completely shift our decision-making mechanism here and stop regarding this as basically a market economic problem."

No, the kind of action needed now harkened back to World War II, Woolsey believed. He once had considered becoming a history professor, and history was his main hobby. Oftentimes he framed modern problems and solutions by the examples of history. In 1942 President Franklin Roosevelt appointed James F. "Jimmy" Byrnes his director of economic stabilization and charged him with mobilizing the wartime economy. Byrnes oversaw retooling of Detroit's factories so that within six months they were producing military transport trucks and other supplies instead of cars. Woolsey paraphrased Byrnes: "I'll make mistakes, but in war, inaction is the greatest of mistakes."

Such radical changes are uncommon in American history and never should be permanent, Woolsey acknowledged, but with, say, a five-year authorization and appropriate sundown legislation, this could be just what we need now. Give somebody the authority to cut through the usual red tape and site new power plants, rebuild energy infrastructure, and move industry to create new kinds of cars and fuels that get the transportation sector off of oil.

Addressing the vulnerabilities of the power grid may be nearly impossible under normal conditions, he argued. You'd have to bring to one table local and US federal regulators, the utilities, and Canadian regulators and utility — because it's all one grid — facing the fear of lawsuits if they don't think of every possible thing that could go wrong, and try to prevent it. Good ideas crop up all the time, yet decisions and changes don't get made because of all this.

Secretary of the Interior Carol Browner cautioned against giving anyone the power to over-ride environmental protections in the pursuit of energy. Woolsey persisted. "For industry to do the sorts of things that we did in World War II, and to move out and do it decisively — now, there is an example for the world. That says the United States is doing something. Releasing a few more barrels from the strategic petroleum reserve does not do that," he said.

Besides, tapping the oil reserve wouldn't solve the problem of future terrorist attacks. Woolsey gave the executive committee a quick rundown on the vulnerabilities of the US domestic energy system.

EASY TARGETS

First, the nuclear plants. Though many of them are reasonably well guarded, they're still vulnerable to unconventional attacks or to having aircraft crash into them, potentially causing a

Chernobyl-type meltdown. "It's not easy to do, but it's not unimaginable," he said.

Another vulnerability in the electrical system was the transformers. Modular, small transformers should be commissioned to have on hand to replace existing transformers in case of attack, he suggested. Typical security around a transformer today consists of a small fence with a sign that says, "Transformer." "If your native language is Arabic, and you've got a handgun, and you only know one English word, "transformer," you're still probably in pretty good shape" to attack the US power grid, Woolsey said.

Power plants besides the nuclear ones have their own problems. Electrical power plants tend to be located in isolated areas, necessitating long transmission lines to get the power to the people who need it. The lines can sag, or get hot and congested, and a line problem in one area can affect many people elsewhere. A fallen tree branch in Ohio struck transmission lines and took out much of the power in the Eastern United States and Canada in the summer of 2004. "Terrorists, unfortunately, are smarter than tree branches," he said.

Liquified natural gas terminals or oil refineries also could be targets of attack. Long pipelines for oil and natural gas crisscross the country, with computer control systems vulnerable to hacking. The loss of one isolated pipeline or transmission line can be repaired fairly quickly. Of more concern are areas or "nodes" where many pipelines, transmission lines, and energy facilities converge.

Much of the US energy infrastructure was built long after the country last faced a foreign invader — the British — in the early 1800s, Woolsey noted. "These networks were pretty much all put together with an eye toward openness, ease of access, low cost, maximum public information, and without a single thought being given to their vulnerabilities."

Creating more local power generators could reduce the chances of a major energy collapse, much in the same way the Internet remains functioning even if a part of it goes down. Woolsey's belief in the value of this distributed generation extends to the solar panels on the roof of his Maryland farmhouse. His environmental instincts led him to install energy-efficient windows, a solar hot-water system, and the 3.75-kW solar electric system that usually covers about a quarter of the home's electrical use but could cover all of it under very frugal conditions.

Although he went solar to please his green side, he liked the national security angle of his solar panels, too. If terrorists attack a large power plant — big disaster. If terrorists have to attack everyone's solar panels — not happening. The more solar panels and windmills the country could install, the better for national security.

Woolsey's Republican friends regarded him as "oddly liberal" on social issues like the environment, and some of his Democratic friends were put off by his hawkish stance of foreign policy. That didn't bother him; he kind of enjoyed being the bad boy of both political parties. He had friends on both sides of the aisle, having served in presidential appointments in two Republican and two Democratic administrations.

A child of conservative Democratic parents in Oklahoma, he became a lawyer and served as undersecretary of the navy. On the side, he did some pro bono work for the Natural Resources Defense Council, filing one of the first legal petitions dealing with emissions of chlorofluorocarbons, which eat up the atmosphere's ozone layer. After his stint as CIA director in 1993–1995, concerns about energy security converged with concerns about global warming. It was easier in the Republican-controlled capital to talk about energy security. Even if you were convinced of global warming, you didn't emphasize it because it usually got you nowhere among conservatives.

Besides, if push came to shove, Woolsey would support new power plant sitings, off-shore drilling, nuclear plants, military intervention in oil-producing nations, or whatever it takes for national security over lesser environmental concerns. One way to avoid a lot of that, he believed, was by freeing America from its dependence on oil.

OPTIONS FOR INDEPENDENCE FROM OIL

After the oil embargo crisis of the 1970s, US electric utilities shifted from using oil to using other energy sources such as coal and natural gas to make electricity. Today, only about 3% of US electricity comes from oil. At the same time, Congress passed legislation that led to a doubling in vehicle fuel economy. All subsequent attempts to improve gas mileage over the next 20-plus years stalled in a political stalemate between environmentalists and the auto and oil industries.

To meet today's challenges, the transportation industry would need to move away from oil, just like the utilities did in the 1970s, he thought.

The executive committee summoned Undersecretary of Energy Joseph Romm to brief them on the options for quickly reducing US demand for oil. Woolsey was pleased to hear Romm's name mentioned. His 2004 report on "The Car and Fuel of the Future: A Technology and Policy Overview" for the National Commission on Energy Policy had introduced Woolsey to plug-in hybrids. Romm had recommended that the government phase in CO_2 emission caps for cars, aggressively pursue plug-in hybrids, aggressively promote production of cellulosic ethanol, and decrease the resources going to hydrogen research. The Commission included these strategies in its final report in December 2004 called "Ending the Energy Stalemate."

Today, however, they needed Romm to give them more immediate options. "I think there's a lot of opportunity," Romm said. He suggested that the president should call on Americans to reduce or combine discretionary car trips, use ride-sharing and carpooling, and obey the speed limit. Simply slowing down from 75 to 65 miles per hour (from 120 to 104 km per hour) would reduce highway gasoline consumption by about 15%. Another 5%–15% could be saved if drivers tuned up their cars and fully inflated their tires. "It might surprise you to know that one quarter of the cars and up to one third of the SUVs on the road have seriously under-inflated tires, which not only hurts their gasoline mileage, it actually makes the cars less safe to drive," Romm explained.

Beefing up mass transit, asking corporations to encourage telecommuting and flexible schedules, and educating the public about the need for sacrifice in wartime could help. All told, these steps and the higher price of gasoline after the Saudi and Alaska attacks could decrease US demand for oil by 2 or 3 million barrels a day. Combined with some release from the strategic petroleum reserve, this could be enough to weather the crisis.

Things could get worse, though, Romm reminded the committee, so it would be wise for the president to formulate plans for mandatory gasoline allocations and alternate drive days in case voluntary measures prove insufficient.

"Voluntary is not going to work," General Kelley groused. "The average American just doesn't volunteer for these kinds of things." He agreed with Woolsey that these exceptional times call for exceptional governmental action. "We are at war. More people died on 9/11 than died at Pearl Harbor. The enemy is far more insidious than anybody we have ever fought."

The patriotic spark in Americans after 9/11 contributed to the soaring popularity of hybrids, Energy Secretary Linda Stuntz countered. "I don't think the folks in Detroit saw it coming, but others did," she said. Tax incentives to move automakers toward cleaner car options could work, she believed.

Woolsey suggested trading the billions of dollars per year in government subsidies that go to the oil industry for subsidies to produce cleaner cars and alternative fuels. Treasury Secretary Don Nickles argued against bold government action like instituting dramatic increases in Corporate Average Fuel Economy (CAFE) standards. Leave these decisions to the marketplace, he suggested. "This isn't the time for us to have a czar that's going to be setting prices or rationing."

Woolsey bristled. "If you look up your history you'll find that Jimmy Byrnes was no czar. He had specific authorities to do crucial things with respect to the war," he said calmly. "If you want to get decisive things done quickly in the midst of a war, if you want to do all of this — encourage hybrids and high-grade diesels and plug-in hybrids and alternative fuels, and get power plants going, and protect the ports and all the rest," a Jimmy Byrnes model will get the job done.

"These attacks have given us an opportunity to grab things, get going, give the president the authority through legislation to make the changes that need to be made," Woolsey pleaded. "If we don't take that route, we're going to be very, very sorry in the future."

THIS TIME, IT'S PRETEND

After five hours of intense discussions, the committee wrapped up its meeting by turning up the lights in the hotel ballroom where they sat, so that committee members could see the audience from the stage. The unrest in Nigeria, the attacks in Alaska and Saudi Arabia — none of it had really happened; this was a war game. Woolsey and eight other former high-level government officials had played the roles assigned them in an "Oil Shockwave" simulation sponsored by the non-profit group Securing America's Future Energy and by the National Commission on Energy Policy. They knew their assigned roles in advance, but not the events or situations they would face. The organizers consulted experts in macroeconomics, national security, and world oil production and distribution to make the fictional scenarios as plausible as possible.

The potential for these kinds of crises, however — and even worse ones — are all too real. Woolsey likes to point to the opening scenario of a 2003 book by former CIA operative Robert Baer, *Sleeping with the Devil: How Washington Sold Our Soul for Saudi Crude.*[3] Terrorists hijack a 747 plane and crash it into sulfur-clearing towers in northeastern Saudi Arabia. Around 67% of all Saudi oil gets processed through one huge facility. That kind of attack could interrupt production of 6 million barrels a day of oil and push oil prices well over $100 per barrel for a year or more while the facility is repaired, wreaking havoc in the world economy.

Or if Saudi dissidents staged multiple attacks on foreign oil workers, prompting foreign contractors to pull personnel out of the country (another scenario discussed during the "Oil Shockwave"), oil prices could shoot to over $150 per barrel.

In the end, Woolsey hadn't convinced his colleagues on the "executive committee" to take the strategic actions he felt were needed for long-term security. Instead, they opted to recommend that the president draw down the strategic petroleum reserve, among other responses.

But outside of the "Oil Shockwave" exercise, like-minded neoconservatives echoed his views, and their voices were beginning to be heard.

CHAPTER 8

Conservatives Chime In

P ROFESSOR ANDREW FRANK approached the intense young man with the frowning demeanor. Frank liked what he'd heard Joe Romm say in his speech that morning to the transportation studies department at the University of California, Davis. Romm was right about the folly of waiting for a hydrogen-powered economy, as far as Frank was concerned. Perhaps, if Romm had time to spare from his 2004 book tour to promote *The Hype About Hydrogen*, Frank could show him a better alternative.

Romm hadn't yet written his influential paper for the National Commission on Energy Policy on the car and fuel of the future when Frank invited him to the laboratory. He gave Romm the full tour of the hangar-like garage full of plug-in hybrid prototypes. The experience was an eye-opener for Romm and ultimately would influence a chain of powerful people in Washington, DC, stretching to the president himself.

An energy consultant who had served in the Clinton administration, Romm had been invited to write a March 2004 background paper on hydrogen for the National Commission on Energy Policy, a two-year-old consensus panel of experts supported by the William and Flora Hewlett Foundation and four other charitable trusts and foundations. Romm proposed that he also write a backgrounder for the commission on "The Car and Fuel of the Future: A Technology and Policy Overview," which he submitted in June 2004. Among Romm's conclusions:

- To reduce US dependence on imported oil and avoid potentially catastrophic consequences of climate change, the US will need to significantly reduce greenhouse gas emissions from the transportation sector by 2025 and drastically reduce them by 2050.
- The only plausible strategy for doing that by 2025 is to improve fuel efficiency, and the most plausible strategy for doing that by 2050 is to promote plug-in hybrid vehicles that run on a combination of electricity made from low-carbon sources and a fuel made from low-carbon biomass, not gasoline.
- The US should phase in standards to reduce carbon dioxide emissions in cars and light trucks by at least 33% per mile for new vehicles in 2020, which still would leave new US vehicles less efficient than European vehicles will be by 2010.
- The US should aggressively pursue plug-in hybrids, which are more efficient and less costly than hydrogen fuel-cell vehicles by a factor of three or four. Plug-in hybrids "are probably the ideal future platform for addressing all three major problems created by current vehicles: greenhouse gas emissions, tailpipe emissions, and oil consumption," he wrote.
- The US should promote fuels made from biomass, the most promising being cellulosic ethanol.
- The US should shift the undeserved attention and funding given to hydrogen toward these other strategies and continue hydrogen research at a lower level as part of a long-term possible energy alternative.

Romm had introduced Woolsey to the idea of plug-in hybrids. Serving on the National Commission on Energy Policy, Woolsey brought an already well-developed knowledge of biomass fuels, especially cellulosic ethanol. As early as 1999, he and Indiana Senator Richard Lugar co-authored an article on "The New Petroleum" in *Foreign Affairs*, and Woolsey had served on the board of a company considering a commercial cellulosic ethanol plant.

But the idea of plug-in hybrids was a new one to Woolsey. Flex-fuel plug-in hybrids became one part of the recommendations made in the commission's final report in December 2004, "Ending the Energy Stalemate: A Bipartisan Strategy to Meet America's Energy Challenges." It was a strategy that got under Woolsey's skin. Here was a quick path away from oil, away from being indebted to hostile countries, away from the gaping vulnerabilities created by our dependence on oil.

Commuting from his farm to his office at the consulting firm Booz Allen Hamilton, Woolsey drove a Toyota Prius, one of two hybrids in his family. The other was one that some people derided as a phony hybrid — a Lexus hybrid SUV with a fuel efficiency that was only one mile per gallon better than a conventional Lexus, in Woolsey's experience. Still, bumper stickers on both cars read, "Osama bin Laden hates this car." That made Woolsey smile.

The idea that we could be getting hundreds of miles per gallon of petroleum with flex-fuel plug-in hybrids could mean an economic hit to Al Qaeda. The Saudis already had given more than $80 billion to spread the Wahhabi doctrine and indirectly helped create terrorists, he believed. Why should US money be part of that? If you want to see a frown on the face of the Wahhabis, show them a plug-in hybrid, thought Woolsey.

In a parallel time frame, Anne Korin, co-director of a Washington, DC-based think-tank focused on national security, traveled west for an informational visit to the Electric Power Research Institute (EPRI). Things had changed for global security experts since September 11, 2001. The alternative-fuel message no longer belonged only to environmentalists. Al Qaeda's attacks made it crystal clear, if it wasn't clear already, that America's security and economic stability were threatened by its dependence on oil.

Korin's organization, the Institute for the Analysis of Global Security (IAGS), was one of several planning to launch a new coalition that she would chair, called Set America Free — as in, free from the bondage of petroleum, free from the foreign masters of oil. Korin was researching liberation strategies. Bob Graham at EPRI told her about plug-in hybrids.

Some of the heavy hitters of hawkish Washington think-tanks and public-policy organizations filled the roster of Set America Free when it launched its "Blueprint for Energy Security" in September 2004: the Foundation for Defense of Democracies; the Center for Security Policy; the Hudson Institute; the National Defense Council, and people like Robert C. "Bud" McFarlane, President Ronald Reagan's national security advisor.

Alongside the neoconservatives in founding Set America Free was the American Council on Renewable Energy. Within a few months, the coalition's "Blueprint" attracted new members, including the Natural Resources Defense Council, the Apollo Project (a labor and business coalition looking toward a sustainable future), anti-feminist and anti-homosexual activist Gary L. Bauer of American Values, the Jewish Institute for National Security Affairs, and James Strock, former California secretary for environmental protection. The "Blueprint" called on Congress to spend $12 billion over four years to cut oil use by half by 2025. That's a lot, but it pales in comparison to other ambitious national undertakings, notes Frank J. Gaffney, Jr., president of the Center for Security Policy and a former Pentagon official under President Ronald Reagan. In today's dollars, the Manhattan Project price tag would be $20 billion, and the Apollo program would be $100 billion.[1]

Oil-related problems have coalesced into a "perfect storm" threatening America, with these key elements: declining oil reserves; economic competition, and ideological warfare, the Blueprint warns.

PEAK OIL

The world is running out of oil, which is a finite resource. How quickly this is happening is a matter of some debate, but there's already consensus that we are very near or already at the peak of world oil production, and that over the next decades less and less will be available. Some unconventional sources of oil might be exploited to help fill the gap, like squeezing oil out of the tar sands of Canada, but getting at those sources is much more expensive and energy intensive and an environmental nightmare.

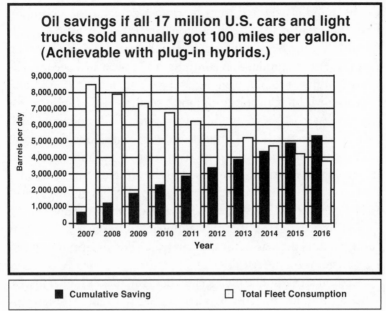

Oil savings if all 17 million U.S. cars and light trucks sold annually got 100 miles per gallon. (Achievable with plug-in hybrids.)

■ Cumulative Saving □ Total Fleet Consumption

Meridian International Research

American geologist M. King Hubbert predicted in 1956 that annual oil production — the amount of oil being pumped out of the ground in any given year — would follow a bell-shaped curve, with production increasing to a peak (now widely known as Hubbert's peak) as new sources are tapped and then declining when all existing sources are being drained. He correctly predicted the US peak of the early 1970s. In 1969 he estimated that there are 2.1 trillion barrels of oil in the world and that production would peak in 2000.[2] Princeton geophysicist Kenneth S. Deffeyes's calculations in 2004 put the total at 2.013 trillion barrels, with production peaking in late 2005 or early 2006.[3] Multiple other experts have made similar predictions.

Regardless of how long you think supplies of oil will last, they're not enough to meet the growing demand. World energy consumption doubled between 1970 and 2002 and is expected to increase by 2% per year over the next 20 years, the US Department of Energy reported in February 2006.[4] Oil consumption nearly doubled and is expected to grow from a demand for 78 million barrels per day in 2002 to 119 million barrels per day in 2025.

In July 2005 Saudi officials admitted that if the gap between demand and oil production continues to grow, it will become extremely difficult to pump enough oil over the next 10 to 15 years.[5]

ExxonMobil Corporation's 2005 report, "The Outlook for Energy: A 2030 View," predicted that world oil production will peak around 2010. US oil imports are expected to double from 10 million barrels per day in 2002 to almost 20 million barrels per day in 2025. Two-thirds of oil used in the United States goes into transportation, mostly cars and trucks. The US has just over 3% of world oil reserves, but we gobble up 25% of the oil produced.

Oil imports aren't the only problem. American natural-gas production is decreasing by 5% per year. Global consumption of natural gas is on the rise.

Less oil and gasoline plus greater demand means higher prices. Already, though, the cost is much higher than most Americans think. The price of a gallon of gasoline at the tank averaged $3 by the summer of 2006, but hidden costs bring its true price to more than double that, the IAGS says.

The oil industry gets billions of dollars worth of federal subsidies each year in the form of tax breaks and government protection programs to help it compete and keep prices low for consumers. ExxonMobil reported $9.9 billion in quarterly profits in late 2005, around the same time that the US Congress voted to give the oil and gasoline industry $10.7 billion in tax breaks over the next five years, the Union of Concerned Scientists reported. Military assistance to Middle East countries and deployment of US forces to secure our access to oil costs about $50 billion per year, not counting the war budgets. Price hikes and interruptions in oil supplies from unstable or hostile countries have cost the US economy more than $7 trillion in today's dollars over the last 30 years, according to a study for the US Department of Energy. The US has sent $4.16 trillion overseas to pay for oil in the past 30 years, accounting for nearly a third of the country's deficit. Because the deficit is linked to unemployment, that has cost millions of US jobs.

Then there's the cost of wars. An oil dispute triggered the 1990–91 Gulf War, which cost the international community close to $80 billion. For the $400 billion (and climbing) cost of the 2003 war in Iraq and the subsequent US occupation, 8 million petroleum-free RAV4-EVs could have been put on US streets (using a high price for each RAV4-EV of $50,000), jumpstarting the plug-in vehicle industry with such vigor that the costs of production would have plummeted.

The National Defense Council Foundation estimates that the real cost of gasoline, if we add in these hidden costs, is more than $5.28 per gallon.

Oil for cars competes with other uses of oil, such as the 90% of organic chemicals that are made from petroleum, for things including pharmaceuticals, plastics, and agricultural chemicals.[6] As Marc Geller says, it's a choice between riding to the store in your Hummer today, or having life-saving medications available to your grandchild.

Plug-in hybrids can cushion the oil crunch. If all cars on the road by 2025 are hybrids and half are plug-in hybrids, we'd only need to import 12 million barrels per day (8 million per day less than predicted), the IAGS estimates. If all these hybrids and plug-in hybrids also are flexible-fuel vehicles, the US would import only 8 million barrels per day in 2025 — less than we import today.

A similar conclusion appeared in a recent issue of a magazine for Tau Beta Pi, a national engineering honor society in the United States. Robert E. Uhrig, Ph.D., professor of nuclear engineering, emeritus, at the University of Tennessee estimated that if all cars and light trucks are plug-in hybrids by 2035, they would replace 281 million gallons of gasoline per day with electricity as fuel. That's equal to 6.7 million barrels of oil, or 74% of the estimated 9 million barrels of oil per day presently used to produce gasoline and diesel fuel for the light-vehicle fleet.[7]

Because older cars on the road stick around even as new cars get introduced, it takes approximately 15 years to replace all the cars and trucks being driven. All the more reason to get started immediately, Korin notes.

ECONOMIC COMPETITION

We're not the only ones who want the dwindling barrels of oil. The fast-growing economies of China and India are bringing much of their immense populations into the middle class with a hunger for the cars and goods that implies. Together these two countries contain a third of the world's population. China's middle class alone is larger than the entire US population, and the country has the fastest-growing auto market. Car sales in China are growing at 50%–60% per year, and energy needs for road transportation are expected to increase by 5% per year between 2004 and 2030, the US Department of Energy reports.[8] China went from being energy self-sufficient in 1985 to importing 1% of its oil in 1993 to importing 48% of its oil in 2004.

Over the next 20 years, China and India may need an additional 40 million barrels per day of oil, which would be a 50% increase from 1995 world production levels and more than twice the growth in world oil production seen over the last 20 years, suggests Gal Luft, executive director of the IAGS.

If the populations of China and India increase as predicted and their per-person energy consumption by 2050 is similar to that of South Korea's today, China and India by themselves would use more oil than the entire world consumed in 2003.[9] Production from China's largest oil field peaked in 1997. Its proven reserves probably won't last more than two more decades. Today China gets 58% of its oil from the Middle East, but that will rise to 70% by 2015. Car-buying fever should give the Chinese more cars than the US by 2030. By that year, China will be importing as much oil as the US imports today, the International Energy Agency estimated.

IDEOLOGICAL WARFARE

In 1996 al Qaeda issued two fatwas (religious rulings) declaring war and jihad against the United States for having soldiers in Saudi Arabia, home of Islam's two holiest places, Mecca and Medina. The US presence in Saudi Arabia has always been because of oil. This led directly to al Qaeda's attacks on September 11.

Who's got oil? Mostly countries that don't like America or are politically unstable. Just counting proven oil reserves, two-thirds are in the Middle East: Saudi Arabia, Iran, and Iraq claim 44% of the total. Outside the Middle East, 80% of proven oil reserves are in countries where radical Islam is on the rise. The rest of the big producers, other than the United States, Canada, and Norway, are politically unstable or not particularly friendly to the United States. Russia has about 5% of proven oil reserves, but its production peaked around 1999. Africa claims about 7% of proven oil reserves. Nigeria, the largest African producer, will hit peak production around 2010.

The price of oil reflects the fact that it's a fungible commodity. Think of it as a big swimming pool; producers pour the oil in, and consumers suck the oil out. We may want to buy oil from country X but not country Y, but country Y can still punish us by withholding oil from the pool, making the price of a barrel go up because there's less oil to meet demand.

If countries outside the Middle East increase oil production in order to minimize the influence of the Arab-dominated Organization of Petroleum Exporting Countries (OPEC), that just means non-OPEC countries will run dry faster, and everyone eventually will be more dependent on OPEC than ever. Even if production continues at today's rate, many of the top producers in 2002 will be irrelevant to oil markets within two decades — countries like the United States, Russia, Mexico, Norway, China, and Brazil, the IAGS estimates.

"OPEC is going to be around for a heck of a long time," Korin says.

China's interest in securing oil supplies provides some protection to countries that the United States has criticized. Attempts to punish Iran for developing its nuclear programs are unlikely to go anywhere because of its energy deals with China and India and the fact that China sits on the United Nations Security Council, according to Korin. Besides, with such a tight world oil market, if Iran decides to flex its muscles and withhold oil, prices could shoot up and wreak economic havoc.

"We have lost our foreign policy leverage over these countries,"

Korin says. "Look at Sudan," where the Islamic government killed more than 2 million Christians and animists in widely condemned genocide. "The United States tried to do something about it, but the most it could get through the UN Security Council was a very weak-kneed kind of statement — 'Sudan, you're behaving very badly!' — because Sudan is a major oil supplier to China. And China's sitting on the Security Council."

The IAGS maintains a database of attacks against critical energy infrastructure worldwide (and makes a portion of that, attacks in Iraq, available on its website). It shows a widespread trend: Terrorists have marked oil as a target. After an attack on the French oil tanker, the *Lindberg*, off Yemen, al Qaeda released a statement saying the mujahaddin attacked the line that feeds the artery of the life of the Crusader nation (meaning America). "They get it," says Korin, "so we need to get it, and we need to act."

An explosion at a British Petroleum oil refinery near Houston in March 2005 killed 15 people and wounded more than 100. Although terrorists were not to blame for the explosion, it set off mental alarm bells in many people who hadn't paid much attention to the vulnerabilities of the US energy system.

Some neoconservatives ramped up activities, both publicly and behind the scenes, to push for oil-independence policies. The Center for Security Policy's Frank Gaffney, a big booster of the war in Iraq, organized a joint letter to President Bush in April 2005 from 31 national security experts on behalf of the Energy Future Coalition, a nonpartisan think-tank. The letter called for mandated increases in fuel-efficiency standards and development of alternative-fuel vehicles.

"The good news is that the solution to getting off oil is at hand," Robert "Bud" McFarlane proclaimed in a media interview.[10] Co-signers included Woolsey, Boyden Gray, who was White House counsel for President H. W. Bush, and Democrats including former Colorado Senator Gary Hart.

Testifying before the US House Committee on Government Reform's Subcommittee on Energy and Resources in the spring of 2005, Woolsey laid out the National Commission on Energy Policy's recommendations:

- Congress should instruct the National Highway Traffic Safety Administration to phase in strengthened Corporate Average Fuel Economy (CAFE) standards over a five-year period starting no later than 2010, but tweak the rules to get them past the long-standing political stalemate over fuel-economy standards. Allow auto manufacturers to trade compliance credits between car and light-truck categories and between companies. Consider capping the cost of the CAFE program, which would give automakers a "safety valve" in case costs are higher than regulators estimate.
- Offer $1.5 billion in tax incentives over a 10-year-period to encourage both domestic and foreign car companies to retool to produce hybrid and advanced diesel vehicles. This should help maintain domestic manufacturing jobs, which would produce enough tax receipts to offset the cost of the incentives, the Commission estimated.
- Emphasize the importance of making plug-in hybrids for greater fuel efficiency and lower fuel costs for consumers.
- Establish a $1.5-billion, 10-year effort to encourage development of domestically produced alternative fuels like cellulosic ethanol and biodiesel. Through targeted support for research and development, plus incentives for pioneer commercial production facilities, the cost of making cellulosic ethanol could be below the cost of corn-based ethanol and close to the cost of gasoline within two decades, the Commission suggested.

The Commission didn't put a dollar figure behind its endorsement of plug-in hybrids mainly because it was under the mistaken impression, in December of 2004, that battery technology wasn't yet up to the task. The media spotlight found the California Cars Initiative (CalCars) PRIUS+ a few months later and widened to include the EnergyCS plug-in Prius, but the battery fallacy persisted in the minds of most national security experts. The early media stories on plug-in hybrids all included standard responses from car company representatives stating that battery technology wasn't good enough for mass production of plug-in hybrids.

Woolsey and Shultz summed things up in a recent policy paper for the Committee on the Present Danger, a group of neoconservatives and like-minded supporters that originated in the 1950s and has come and gone twice since then, always taking a conservative view of defense and foreign policy issues. Woolsey and Shultz resurrected the Committee in its current incarnation to focus on energy issues. Their June 2005 paper, officially titled "Oil and Security, a Committee on the Present Danger Policy Paper," began, "This paper could well be called, 'It's the Batteries, Stupid.'"[11]

"By most assessments, some battery development will be necessary" to bring plug-in hybrids to market, they wrote. Battery development deserves the highest priority "because it promises to revolutionize transportation economics and to have a dramatic effect on the problems caused by oil dependence." In the meantime, immediate policy steps could include support for "available technologies" including hybrids, modern diesel vehicles, and use of lightweight carbon-fiber composite materials in vehicle construction, Woolsey and Shultz suggested. Combine these with cellulosic ethanol, or biodiesel (especially if made from wastes), and the oil-saving advantages build on themselves.

A hybrid that gets 50 miles (80 km) per gallon could get 100 miles (160 km) per gallon if made from carbon composites that would be lighter but no more expensive than conventional materials, they wrote. Run that lightweight hybrid on 85% cellulosic ethanol or a similar proportion of biodiesel, and it would get hundreds of miles per gallon of gasoline or petroleum-derived fuel. Upgrade that car to a plug-in hybrid that runs 30 miles (48 km) on electricity before tapping the liquid fuel, and it might get 1,000 miles (1,600 km) per gallon of gasoline. All of this could fit into the existing infrastructure without requiring major changes from consumers.

"What are we waiting for?" Woolsey and Shultz asked.

The hawks' advocacy for plug-in hybrids was all the more notable because, for most of them, it was a leap of faith. Woolsey, for one, had never been in a plug-in car, much less driven one. But that was about to change.

THE PEOPLE'S LEAGUE

CHAPTER 9

From the CIA to PIA

C HELSEA SEXTON GRIMACED. There was that same tired
line that the major automakers loved: The batteries aren't
ready. The batteries aren't ready. We don't have electric cars or
plug-in hybrids because the batteries aren't good enough yet.

This time the person saying it was Jim Woolsey.

The Oil Shockwave war game in DC had generated so much
media coverage that organizers scheduled a second one in the
Torrance, California, Civic Center in August of 2005. Once
again, Woolsey urged freedom from oil as the path to national
security, using readily available technology that's compatible with
the existing infrastructure.

"We've wasted too much time and effort on hydrogen fuel
cells," he said. "Hybrids, high-grade diesels, cellulosic ethanol,
and biodiesel not just from soy but from animal wastes are already
on the market. We're not talking about some type of Manhattan
Project to invent something big and new. We're talking about encouraging things that are either here or — in the case of improved
batteries for plug-in hybrids — very, very nearly here."

Sexton had seen the paper by Woolsey and Shultz on "It's the
Batteries, Stupid," and it peeved her. Maybe this guy Woolsey
was new to the topic and didn't know that batteries already had

proved themselves, but Shultz should know better, she thought. Shultz had leased one of her babies, an EV1, both the early version with lead-acid batteries and the later EV1 with nickel-metal hydride (NiMH) batteries.

Chelsea and Bob Sexton had come to the Oil Shockwave on the spur of the moment after getting a call from Paul Scott. They met up with Scott, who drove there in an electric RAV4-EV, and with Greg Hanssen, who came in the EnergyCS plug-in Prius. They didn't know much about the event but knew that Woolsey would be there and that he was an advocate for plug-in hybrids. What a disappointment to hear him bad-mouth batteries.

As the Oil Shockwave wrapped up, the organizers announced that the press conference would begin in the courtyard momentarily, featuring hybrid cars and prototype fuel-cell vehicles. Chelsea followed Woolsey out to the courtyard and approached him, feeling a bit self-conscious as the only person wearing blue-jeans in a crowd full of suits.

"Your partner had one of my cars," she said. Woolsey looked at her, uncomprehending. Chelsea wasn't sure if he'd hear her out, or call security.

"George Shultz drove an EV1," she said. Woolsey didn't quite know what she meant. He wasn't entirely sure what an EV1 was.

"By the time Mr. Shultz had to give up his electric car, the EV1 was using nickel-metal hydride batteries, which easily could power the kind of plug-in hybrids that you're talking about," she said pleasantly. Woolsey's eyes lit up now in recognition, and he smiled.

Chelsea seized the moment. "Why did you two write in your paper on 'It's the Batteries, Stupid' that battery technology needs more R&D to be ready for plug-in hybrids? We've got a plug-in hybrid outside right now that's getting 100 miles per gallon. Plus an all-electric SUV that can go 120 miles on a charge."

Woolsey chimed in: "Yes, I've been reading a bit about electric cars in the news. Seems there are some people here in California who've been out demonstrating in front of dealerships and getting celebrities involved, and so on, trying to save the last remaining electric cars."

Chelsea and Bob exchanged a quick laugh with Scott. "We *are* those people," she said with a smile.

She started to tell him about Southern California Edison's fleet of RAV4-EVs, and how they had done extensive real-world testing on NiMH batteries, and how they'd been proving to be reliable after 100,000 miles (160,000 km) and years of driving. Sexton sensed the Oil Shockwave handlers hovering near them, waiting to move Woolsey toward the press conference.

"If you do nothing else, you must take a test ride in the plug-in hybrid that's out in the parking lot before you go. The thing you've been talking about — it's here, outside. It's not flex-fuel, but otherwise it's what you're talking about," she said.

"Okay," Woolsey said. "I've got this press conference to go to, but afterwards we'll do that. And since you're the one making me do it, you have to go too."

Chelsea smiled. "Deal."

Out in the parking lot later, they talked for a long time amid a larger group of people gathered around Hanssen's plug-in Prius and Scott's RAV4-EV. Sexton, Scott, and Hanssen schooled them as quickly as they could about the grassroots battles in California to stop car makers from destroying the electric cars that customers loved, about the vigils and the protests, the victories and defeats. They wanted the East Coast groups that were pushing for plug-in hybrids as a theoretical concept to know that West Coast groups were doing the same thing, but from a more practical standpoint, because they had the cars.

Looking over the plug-in Prius, Woolsey asked Hanssen, "Can we go for a ride?" Two other participants in the Shockwave got in the back seats, and Hanssen and Woolsey got in front. They started to pull away, but Woolsey said, "Wait." He opened the door, slid up one side of the bucket seat and waved Sexton over. "Get in," he said. If anyone was going to tell him about the pros and cons of this car, it would be this knowledgeable former GM employee, even if they had to squeeze in together. Sexton crunched in next to him on the other half of the seat.

It was the beginning of an unusual but fruitful alliance between the electric-vehicle activists and the neoconservatives.

After the test ride and more conversation, Woolsey said he had to leave for Los Angeles International Airport. Paul Scott hesitated for a nanosecond before offering Woolsey a ride to the airport in his RAV4-EV. Normally, there would be little chance of Scott and Woolsey sharing anything. Their political views were that different, but here was common ground — plug-in hybrids; electric cars. Woolsey had the clout to help make them happen, and there's nothing like a ride in a good electric car to help people "get" the idea. It's called the EV grin: ride in one, and suddenly the quiet comfort and practicality of electric vehicles seems so obvious that people can't help smiling.

"The airport is on my way back to Santa Monica. I'll give you a lift," Scott offered. During the drive, he told Woolsey how activists just in the past month had convinced Toyota to stop destroying the remaining RAV4-EVs — the latest and greatest success of DontCrush.com.

After the campaigns to save the Th!nks and Rangers, and the frustrating vigil to save the EV1s, DontCrush.com had turned its attention to Toyota.

ET TU, TOYOTA?

The company sold about 400 RAV4-EVs in 2002, a process that it expected to take two years but which took only eight months, after which Toyota stopped taking orders. Those were a minority; close to 1,000 of the RAV4-EVs had been leased. Before 2002 Toyota signed only commercial leases, so individuals intent on getting an electric vehicle formed "boutique" companies that leased one or a handful of RAV4-EVs each. Activists challenged Toyota to prove its contention that there was no market for electric vehicles by offering them for sale, and for a brief time, it did. While the company sold RAV4-EVs in 2002, it also expanded leases to individuals, not just companies.

Toyota offered individual leaseholders the option to buy the SUV at the end of the lease. Not so for the commercial leases, however. Toyota was refusing to renew commercial leases, and rounding up those RAV4-EVs to be destroyed.

DontCrush.com negotiated with Toyota behind the scenes for

months to no avail. In June 2005, activists took to the streets. In Southern California, they gathered outside Toyota dealers on Saturdays with picket signs and informational flyers. They rallied outside Toyota's North American headquarters in Torrance. In Northern California, they dogged Toyota displays of hydrogen fuel-cell prototypes at the United Nations World Environment Day festivities in front of San Francisco City Hall. At the Green Cities Expo, they displayed the California Cars Initiative (Cal-Cars) PRIUS+ and urged attendees to stop by the Toyota booth and ask them why they were crushing the RAV4-EVs.

Just as the campaign to save the Ranger trucks had Dave and Heather to make the story real and personal, the RAV4-EV campaign had its own poster children: Howard Stein and Linda Nicholes. The married couple from Long Beach, California, both drove RAV4-EVs, but Howard had an individual lease, while Linda's was a commercial lease. Howard could buy his RAV4-EV, but Linda couldn't buy hers. Activists handed out hundreds of DontCrush.com flyers showing a happy Howard and a frowning Linda under the headline, "Toyota — Don't crush Linda's car!"

This time, the DontCrush.com campaign generated endorsements from the environmental heavyweights — Sierra Club, Natural Resources Defense Council, and Union of Concerned Scientists — as well as from politicians and the California Environmental Protection Agency.

At their protests and street actions, DontCrush.com activists handed out hundreds of the flyers. Thousands of people around the globe saw the flyers on the Web, translated into Spanish, French, German, Russian, Chinese, and Vietnamese. Marc Geller created a digital animation gif file that mimicked the company's slogan, "Toyota: Moving Forward" and said instead, "Toyota: Moving Backward" before morphing into "Don't Crush Linda's Car!" and finally, "DontCrush.com." Dozens of websites adopted "Toyota: Moving Backward," where a click drove viewers to the DontCrush.com site for the full story.

The news media began paying attention. How could a company that claimed the green high ground with its Prius justify destroying its only zero-emission vehicle when buyers were eager for them? Used Toyota RAV4-EVs were selling on eBay for more than the original retail price. Toyota officials denied that the SUVs were being destroyed and said that the company was donating them to national parks and non-profit agencies. But DontCrush.com activists saw returned RAV4-EVs at a Toyota facility that were marked as if for disposal, with air bags intentionally exploded. They watched and eventually saw a truck loaded with RAV4-EVs leaving the grounds.

Linda Nicholes and Doug Korthoff followed in Linda's RAV4-EV. Where would these electric vehicles end up? In desert crushing grounds, like the EV1? They followed the truck down the 405 Freeway, and onto the 710, headed toward Long Beach, the shipping capital of the Los Angeles region. Eventually the semi pulled onto industrial grounds, and workers closed a chain-link fence hung with a Toyota sign. Linda and Doug could go no further. On the fenced lot next to it, oil wells served as sentries, slowly and rhythmically rearing up and falling, pumping black fossil crude out of the ground. The fate of these RAV4-EVs couldn't be verified.

By July Toyota agreed to stop destroying the commercially leased RAV4-EVs. The company wouldn't sell them, but neither would it crush them. Commercial leases could be extended indefinitely at the preference of the leaseholder. Although Toyota sold Linda Nicholes her RAV4-EV, which she first got on a boutique commercial lease, the company refused to sell the vehicles to other individuals with boutique commercial leases, disappointing many drivers.

After the long, hard slog of the EV1 vigil, the relative ease of the Toyota victory caught DontCrush.com members by surprise. They were ecstatic, even though it wasn't a perfect victory. This called for a celebration.

THE NEXT STAGE

Thirty-some DontCrush.com leaders gathered in the August heat of the Sierra Mountains foothills for a party at Dave and Heather's solar-powered ranch. Two groups carpooled in RAV4-EVs, stopping at an RV park along the way to recharge during the

200+ miles (320+ km) from the San Francisco Bay Area to the ranch. Once the sun set and the summer heat started to lift, Dave fired up the barbecue. Neighbors came by and got their first ride in an electric car. A bluegrass band set up on the back patio and kept toes tapping as the DontCrush.com activists sat out under the stars and got to know each other a bit. Most of them had never met face-to-face. They slept that night in tents or in sleeping bags on the living room floor.

The party was meant to celebrate the past. In the sharp sunlight of the following day, a bit groggy and tired, the group faced the inevitable question. What about the future? What next? They had saved all of the electric cars that they could save. No major car company was going to make a new one any time soon. How could they get more electric vehicles on the road?

A three-hour session of brainstorming and strategizing led to a new direction. Clearly, DontCrush.com was no longer a useful name. Henceforth, the group would be called Plug In America, a name that encompassed both plug-in hybrids and electric vehicles. They would advocate for the use of plug-in cars, trucks, and SUVs powered by cleaner, cheaper, domestic electricity to reduce US dependence on petroleum and improve the global environment.

While they met, Hurricane Katrina ravaged New Orleans, breaching the earthen levees that separated the city from Lake Pontchartrain and the Mississippi River and flooding 80% of the metropolis. It was the fifth hurricane of the 2005 season, in which an extraordinary number of powerful storms and hurricanes illustrated the devastating changes ahead with global warming. Katrina killed more than 1,000 people in New Orleans alone, and 1.5 million Southerners fled or were evacuated from their homes. Much of the area still lies in ruins. Thousands of buildings lost power for weeks at a time. The hurricane flooded a Texas oil refinery and damaged offshore oil drilling platforms.

Four days later, Plug In America held its first press conference call, to announce the Toyota victory and to introduce Plug In America. Woolsey joined in, at Sexton's invitation, and pointed out Hurricane Katrina's lesson on US energy vulnerability. Oil supplies are too tight to lose production and refinery capacity from a natural disaster or man-made attack without taking an economic hit. The US would be wise to pursue more distributed generation of energy to avoid widespread collapse if a centralized power source goes out, he said.

A report released a few weeks earlier by Meridian International Research predicted that global oil production would peak in 2007 or 2008 at the latest, and that by 2010, demand for petroleum would outstrip supply by 10%.[1] "We are facing the Peak Oil Emergency," the authors stated. After an extensive review of the options for coping with decreasing oil supplies, they concluded, "It is clear that the Plug-In Hybrid car is overwhelmingly the best existing solution to declining oil supplies."

That fall Plug In America joined the Set America Free coalition, strengthening the connection between the national security groups and the plug-in activists.

WORKING TOGETHER

Woolsey's consulting work took him to Northern California in October, and he invited Sexton to set up opportunities for him to learn more about the state of battery technology and the possibilities for plug-in hybrids, in between his business meetings. For a week Sexton accompanied him to meetings throughout the San Francisco and Sacramento areas, pointing out electric vehicles every time one passed them by. One important stop: Andrew Frank's garage.

"Andy, as far as I'm concerned, is really the heart of understanding the technology," Woolsey says. "When Andy has cars that can go 60 miles on a charge, and you can kick the tires, it's hard to refute" that plug-in hybrids are here and now.

They met with Alan Lloyd, former chair of the California Air Resources Board and then head of the State Environment Protection Agency, and went on to visits with the California Electric Transportation Coalition and nine non-governmental organizations in the state capital — the Coalition for Clean Air, and others.

Marc Geller met them in San Francisco and drove them in his electric RAV4-EV to meetings with the Union of Concerned

Scientists, the Natural Resources Defense Council, and other groups. Geller hoped that driving all over in his electric SUV would impress upon Woolsey the viability of the NiMH batteries. When they stopped to get a bite for lunch, Geller parked in a city-owned garage that offered charging stations for electric vehicles. His car had plenty of juice, but he plugged in anyway, just to show it off.

Over sandwiches, the three of them chatted amiably — surprisingly amiably, Geller thought, considering how weird it felt to be hanging out with an ex-CIA director. But it was clear in their discussions that they agreed about the need for plug-in hybrids and electric vehicles. Sitting back in a café chair, Geller grinned at Woolsey and Sexton. His friends and family would have a hard time believing this meeting happened. "An ex-CIA chief and me — strange bedfellows," he told Woolsey. "But since you 'came out' for plug-ins, I take great pleasure in citing a hawk in defense of my not-quite-mainstream views."

"Ha!" Woolsey nodded, one side of his mouth rising in a half-smile that looked for a second like Dick Cheney's. "You want strange bedfellows? I think soon we'll have a new group alongside us backing plug-in hybrids — evangelical Christians. I'm sort of an old-fashioned Presbyterian. I look downright middle-of-the-road next to them. But there's a growing movement among the evangelicals for what they call 'creation care.'"

WHAT WOULD JESUS DRIVE?

One line in the Bible is the focus of creation care, Genesis 2:15: "And the Lord God took the man, and put him into the Garden of Eden to dress it and to keep it." That sentence has inspired a significant number of postmillennial evangelicals, who make up the majority of the Christian evangelical movement, to become environmentalists without having to call themselves that.

Most non-evangelicals are more familiar with the minority premillennial evangelicals, like Pat Robertson, James Dobson, and Jerry Falwell. The premillennials believe that Armageddon is imminent, that we are entering the End Times when Jesus returns to earth and fights various battles against evil. A subset of premillennials believes that good Christians will be plucked from the earth and held safe — known as the Rapture — while all this is going on. After the battles are over, the world will enjoy a thousand years of peace.

For the postmillennials, however, this scenario is backward. Genesis 2:15 instructs humans to take good care of the Earth, God's creation, and work to make the world a better place. After we have 1,000 good years of that, Jesus will return. It's a doctrine that charges people to do something, to be active and take responsibility for ecological health, not unlike the Hebrew phrase, "tikkun olam" (meaning repair the world), which has been embraced by many progressive American Jews.

That month, Woolsey was featured in *Audubon Magazine* alongside one of the leading proponents of creation care, Richard Cizik, in an article entitled, "The Holy and the Hawks." Cizik, the political point man for the 30-million-member National Association of Evangelicals (NAE), was described as a pro-Bush, conservative Republican and a devoted foot soldier of the religious right, hell-bent on stopping abortion, same-sex marriage, and embryonic stem-cell research.[2] But he also was very concerned about car exhaust and pollution destroying God's creation.

In 2004 the NAE adopted an ecologically minded charter for the first time in its 63-year history, urging the government to encourage fuel efficiency, reduce pollution, encourage sustainable use of natural resources, and provide for the proper care of wildlife and their natural habitats.

Cizik is mindful of evangelicals' place in history. "It was to our discredit that evangelicals didn't join [Dr. Martin Luther] King in the civil rights movement. It was forever a black mark on us that we weren't part of that," he told the magazine. Cizik wants evangelicals engaged in environmental issues partly so that they will not repeat the mistake of sitting on the sidelines when moral history is being made.

All of which was good news to Woolsey. "If the evangelicals come into this in a big way — and it looks to me like there's a pretty good chance of this — that completely changes the politics. This is an alliance we want," he told Geller and Sexton. "It's pretty clear that most of the major political transformations in American history have in one way or another been rooted in church movements."

LAWMAKERS BEGIN TO LISTEN

Getting America to adopt plug-in hybrids would require transformations great and small, but they were happening. One had happened already in Woolsey. Thanks to Sexton and Geller and Felix Kramer and Andrew Frank and many others, he now understood that battery technology *is* advanced enough for plug-in hybrids.

Testifying before the US Senate Committee on Foreign Relations on November 16, 2005, Woolsey spoke of the "High Cost of Crude: The New Currency of Foreign Policy." Much of his remarks repeated points made in his paper with Shultz, but he rewrote the conclusions about batteries. "Other experts," he noted, "argue that battery development will be necessary" for plug-in hybrids to be viable. "But the California experience with electric vehicles in the 1990s suggests otherwise." Whether what remains is a need for improvements to lithium-ion (Li-ion) batteries or simply financial incentives to mass produce NiMH and Li-ion batteries, "such efforts should have the highest priority," he testified.

A bipartisan group of senators and Congressional representatives, groomed by Set America Free, introduced legislation that month to offer sticks and carrots to start weaning the US transportation sector off oil. Conservative Democratic Senator Joseph Lieberman co-sponsored the Vehicle and Fuel Choices for American Security Act with conservative Republican Senator Sam Brownback of Kansas, along with eight other senators spread out across the political spectrum, including the latest liberal Democratic darling, Senator Barack Obama of Illinois. Earlier that year, Obama had inserted a provision in the federal Energy Bill, which was passed and signed by the president that summer, to provide $40 million for research on plug-in hybrids and flex-fuel vehicles. The Energy Bill also authorized $200 million for Clean Cities pilot programs to buy and support alternative-fuel vehicles at 30 demonstration sites. One section of the Bill called for creation of a Set America Free commission to recommend steps for achieving energy self-sufficiency within North America by 2025.

The Vehicle and Fuel Choices for American Security Act would make it national policy to cut US oil consumption by 10 million barrels per day within 25 years. As introduced, the Bill would require 10 percent of all vehicles sold in the United States to be hybrids, plug-in hybrids, or biofuel or alternative-fuel vehicles by 2012, with that percentage rising by 10 percent per year until half of all vehicles sold in 2016 incorporate these energy alternatives. The Bill also would require that 75 percent of federal fleet purchases by 2016 meet those categories.

Similar legislation introduced simultaneously in the House drew the bipartisan backing of 43 Representatives.

Meanwhile, the media continued to introduce plug-in hybrids to more and more Americans. An Associated Press story landed on more than 150 websites. Reuters, *BusinessWeek* magazine, the *Los Angeles Times, Time* magazine, the *Christian Science Monitor, Popular Mechanics* magazine, and many others ran stories that focused on or included plug-in hybrids. CBS *National News* aired a segment on the EnergyCS plug-in Prius, and National Public Radio's "Science Friday," explored plug-in hybrids. Influential *New York Times* columnist Thomas L. Friedman became an enthusiastic plug-in-hybrid advocate.

Casaba Csere, editor-in-chief of *Car and Driver* magazine, wrote a column asking, "Are plug-in hybrids the next big thing?" and concluding that the jury is still out. In Salon.com's list of the most exciting ideas to help the environment, plug-in hybrids were number 2, behind nanosolar technology in the top spot. *Rolling Stone* teamed with *Salon* for an online special report that included Woolsey in a list of 25 "Climate Warriors and Heroes."

Altogether, plug-in hybrids appeared in the media more than 130 times in 2005 (averaging once every three days), including newspapers in at least 24 cities in the United States, England, France, and Australia. Online, more than 35 news sites and blogs discussed plug-in hybrids, such as HybridCars.com, Smart-Money.com, AlterNet.com, EVWorld.com, the DailyKos, engadget, treehugger, and others.

Environmental media began to pay more attention, with articles in *Solar Today, Mother Earth News, Plenty, Homepower,* and E-magazines, among others.

While the CalCars PRIUS+ and the EnergyCS plug-in Prius were in the news, Felix and Ron moved beyond the Prius. A benefactor donated one of the first hybrid Ford Escape SUVs, and Ron set to work designing its conversion to a plug-in.

After a lengthy search, Ron also found a source for NiMH batteries — Electro Energy, a Connecticut public company with innovative bipolar battery technology. CalCars and Electro Energy made plans to put the company's NiMH batteries into a plug-in Prius.

Sexton spoke alongside some of the other heavy-hitters for plug-in hybrids at a two-day "PHEV Symposium" in November 2005, in Los Angeles organized by the American Public Power Association, a group of publicly owned utilities. Austin Energy's Roger Duncan, Mark Duvall of the Electric Power Research Institute (EPRI), Anne Korin of Set America Free, Greg Hanssen of EnergyCS, and Southern California Edison's Dean Taylor and Ed Kjaer filled the program, among others.

Market introduction of plug-in hybrids is attainable by 2008, EPRI's Duvall said at the symposium.

In the four years before 2005, there were four public workshops on plug-in hybrids. In 2005 alone, there were four more, including a full-day track at the annual meeting of the Electric Drive Transportation Association (EDTA) in December in Vancouver, Canada. The EDTA is unique in including both the major automakers and electrical utilities on its board of directors. This was the first time it had included plug-in hybrids as an official section of the program, and 15 speakers covered everything from the technology to environmental benefits to the cost of plug-in hybrids. The organizers had to pull in extra chairs to seat the standing-room-only crowd, while some seats in the hydrogen fuel-cell section remained empty.

EPRI's Bob Graham recalled speaking about plug-in hybrids at an EDTA conference years earlier. "I was the only speaker on plug-in hybrids. I think I was between motorcycles and fork-lifts" on the program, he said. "We've come a long way since then."[3]

COSTING IT OUT

Graham laughs when he talks about whether or not consumers will want plug-in hybrids, because his wife is a good example of what buyers are willing to pay for the car "values" that they like. His wife drives a Ford Explorer, but not just any Explorer. "She had to have the Eddie Bauer version, because it has the compass and the leather seats. That version is a $35,000 version versus a standard $28,000 version," he said.

Graham's wife, he added, drives about 7 miles (11 km) per day. In a plug-in hybrid, that could be all-electric driving, and she'd almost never buy gasoline.

The extra value of plug-in hybrids — less cost for fuel, reduced pollution, convenient home charging, weaning America off of oil, and the patriotic impulse to improve national security — surely will appeal to a large segment of the public.

A plug-in hybrid with enough batteries for a 20-mile electric range would end up costing the driver the same amount as a conventional gasoline car over a 10-year time span, assuming that gasoline costs $2.25/gallon, electricity costs 8 cents/kWh, and batteries cost $600/kWh, Dean Taylor of Southern California Edison reported at the EDTA.

The price of either NiMH or Li-ion batteries for plug-in hybrids should hit that $600/kWh mark if only 1,000 are manufactured each year, according to an EPRI chart that Taylor showed. At volumes of 10,000 batteries/year, the cost drops to around $400/kWh. Increase battery production so that their cost drops to $300/kWh, and the plug-in hybrid driver would save $2,500 during that 10 years compared with driving a conventional car, Taylor added.

If manufacturers made 100,000 batteries per year, a plug-in hybrid would cost its owner less overall even if gasoline prices fell to $2/gallon. And if gasoline prices rise to $4/gallon, the plug-in hybrid will save its owner $7,000 in 10 years of driving compared with owning a conventional car, he said.

Hybrids would save owners money, too, and reduce pollution compared with conventional cars, but not as much as plug-in hybrids in either case, he calculated. Once sales of both kinds of vehicles reach 100,000/year, hybrid sedans and SUVs will sell for $1,500–$2,400 less than plug-in hybrids that have a 20-mile electric range on NiMH batteries, but the hybrids still will cost more during a 10-year life span because they rely on gasoline.

BATTERIES CAN DO IT

Speakers presented separate findings from EPRI, Southern California Edison, battery-maker Saft, and consultants Tiax LLC that NiMH batteries can meet the technological challenges of plug-in hybrid propulsion today, and Li-ion batteries probably will. Testing, both in lab and real-world settings, shows that NiMH batteries can provide 3,000 cycles of deep discharging and last at least 10 years, reported Marcus Alexander of EPRI. By December of 2005, EPRI had tested Li-ion batteries successfully up to 2,500 deep-discharge cycles, and others had shown 3,300 deep-discharge cycles. Testing for both kinds of batteries was conducted at an average temperature of 77° Fahrenheit (25° Celsius); cycle lives would be shorter at higher temperatures, Alexander noted.

The bottom line: NiMH batteries should provide a 40-mile electric range in plug-in hybrids, and Li-ion batteries show great potential for providing longer than a 40-mile electric range. NiMH batteries have lasted 10 years and at least 3,000 deep-discharge cycles. Li-ion batteries have a 5-year track record and look good so far. Improvements continue to be made in cycle life and calendar life of batteries.

All the formal testing is in addition to the real-world experience of Frank's plug-in hybrids. "We don't think we need to demonstrate umpteen vehicles. That's already been done by Andy Frank for years," Brian Stokes of Pacific Gas and Electric Co. said at the meeting.

"It is not a technical hurdle that stops us from bringing plug-in hybrid electric vehicles to the marketplace," Graham concluded.

Representatives of the major car companies studiously avoided talking about plug-in hybrids during a luncheon panel discussion at the EDTA meeting, focusing on hybrids, fuel-cell vehicles, and neighborhood electric vehicles instead. When pressed by the audience, some said their companies were keeping all options open, but that the technology was very expensive or not ready for production.

The panel was moderated by Robert Stempel, former chairman of General Motors and now CEO of Energy Conversion Devices (ECD), the NiMH battery-maker whose booth at the EDTA displayed a 43-Ah battery that looked suitable for a plug-in hybrid. A veteran of many EDTA meetings, Stempel pointed out the key difference between what the auto company representatives had said during the luncheon compared with past years:

> The interesting thing today was that we didn't hear about battery failure. We didn't hear about motor problems. We didn't hear about system issues. The technology is here. Electric drive is really here. This stuff is reliable, and it works.

As 2006 dawned, however, car company representatives still were telling the media and the public that battery technology wasn't ready for plug-in hybrids.

Thanks to the alliance between the activists and the hawks, that argument no longer works with Woolsey. "I've become very skeptical of the people who say we really have to do some very basic research" before plug-in hybrids are viable, he says today. "If you're willing to go with NiMH, it sure doesn't look to me like we need any R&D. Seems like we need some crescent wrenches" to get to work.

CHAPTER 10

A Convergence of Forces

JANUARY 24, 2006 was an auspicious day for plug-in hybrids. At the Sundance Film Festival in Park City, Utah, audiences packed one of four premier screenings of *Who Killed the Electric Car?* Most of Plug In America was there — Sexton, Geller, Scott, the Raboys, Howard Stein and Linda Nicholes, Rainforest Action Network's Jennifer Krill, and others. The documentary tracks the many unnecessary and untimely deaths of electric cars produced under California's Zero-Emission Vehicle (ZEV) Mandate. Ultimately, the filmmakers suggest that there is "life after death" in the coming of plug-in hybrids.[1]

That same day, the *New York Times* editorialized about ailing Ford Motor Company's plans to eliminate 30,000 jobs and to close up to 14 factories. Among the newspaper's advice: "Ford should be putting more into developing plug-in hybrid vehicles, which can be plugged into the electricity grid, and a lot less into gasoline-guzzling sport utility vehicles."[2]

Elsewhere, two companies announced a partnership to develop a plug-in hybrid drivetrain that could allow a four-passenger sedan to get 250 miles (400 km) per gallon or SUVs to get 150 miles (240 km) per gallon. AFS Trinity Power Corp., based in Bellevue, Washington, brings to the partnership its Extreme Hybrid™ technology, which combines a Li-ion battery pack with a bank of ultracapacitors. The other company, Ricardo Engineering, is a key contractor for Ford, GM, and Hyundai, building transmissions, drivelines, engines, software, and vehicle integration systems. If they succeed, and a major manufacturer licenses their product, their plug-in hybrid design could save drivers between $11,000 and $22,000 in 10 years of fueling costs compared with conventional cars, AFS Trinity officials estimate.

While all this was happening, Austin's Roger Duncan led a press conference in Washington, DC, featuring Woolsey, Frank, Romm, Frank Gaffney of the Center for Security Policy, Republican Senator Orrin Hatch of Utah, and others who gathered for the official launch of Plug-in Partners. Duncan had been stumping around the country for nearly a year, speaking to the US Conference of Mayors, testifying with Gaffney before Congressional subcommittees, and meeting individually with government and business officials to drum up support for plug-in hybrids.

Plug-in Partners aimed to get the 50 largest US cities to replicate the Plug-in Austin program that asks citizens to sign petitions calling for plug-in hybrids and sets aside City money to provide financial incentives for buyers once plug-in hybrids hit the market. Through Austin, Plug-in Partners is collecting "soft" orders for plug-in hybrids for government and commercial fleets; they can't place hard orders until they know what their budgets look like when the vehicles become available, but they usually honor their soft orders. Plug-in Partners aims to prove that there *is* demand for plug-in hybrids, effectively removing one excuse used by automakers for not producing them.

By June 2006, Plug-in Partners had been joined by 29 major US cities, 17 counties and local governments, the State of Minnesota, 26 national and local environmental groups, 33 other non-profits, 3 national security organizations, 137 public power utilities, 2 national utility associations, the 2 largest US biofuel organizations, and 2 Canadian energy companies. Duncan expected to have all 50 cities aboard by the end of 2006. He had amassed fleet orders for 6,000 plug-in hybrids. "I haven't run into opposition from anyone," Duncan says.

Notably, the campaign was being led by cities and publicly owned utilities, not by private utilities. "Our profits go into the parks and libraries of Austin, Texas," Duncan points out. "Our citizens like the idea of wind powering cars." Also notably, the environmental groups supporting Plug-in Partners did not yet include the Sierra Club, Natural Resources Defense Council, or Union of Concerned Scientists. "They are supportive of plug-in hybrids, but they're not joining the campaign officially, saying it isn't their highest priority," he adds.

The January launch drew coverage from the *Wall Street Journal,* the *Los Angeles Times,* MSNBC, and others. Woolsey had this advice for reporters: "If I were to leave you with six words to remember from what I'm saying here, with respect to any of the values that we've been talking about, and the importance of moving away from oil, they're these: Forget hydrogen. Forget hydrogen. Forget hydrogen."

Southern California Edison's Ed Kjaer related how the utility's remaining fleet of 220 RAV4-EVs collectively had driven almost 12 million miles (19 million km) with no major problems in their nickel-metal hydride (NiMH) batteries.

Kateri Callahan, president of the Alliance to Save Energy, put it this way: "Even drawing from our existing power plants, plug-in vehicles have the potential to cut a vehicle's petroleum consumption by three-fourths or more, can operate at as little as one-fourth the fuel cost, and reduce greenhouse gases by two-thirds."

When journalists phoned the car companies for comment, they heard a different story. In separate interviews, Toyota spokespeople Cindy Knight and Bill Kwong regurgitated doubts about the environmental benefits of plug-in cars, saying the electricity comes from fossil fuel-burning power plants. GM spokesmen said the company was looking for a breakthrough in better batteries, and that plug-in hybrid technology was not ready for assembly lines.

The automakers' arguments seemed stuck in time, and yet they had shifted noticeably in the year since plug-in hybrids went public. Company spokespeople initially told the media that plug-in hybrids were not going to happen. Later, they softened their messages to say that they were "studying" the issue and "considering all options." Some even admitted that they could build plug-in hybrids if they wanted to. But always they followed those statements with the same old caveats: The batteries aren't ready. Consumers don't want plug-in hybrids. Plug-in cars pollute more because of power plants.

Despite the automakers' naysaying, momentum for plug-in hybrids hit an all-time high that January 24, 2006. And the fun was only beginning.

INDUSTRY

The Extreme Hybrid™ partnership was significant for bringing in a big automotive player like Ricardo, but there was lots of movement going on in other corners of the car industry.

Earlier that month, Johnson Controls, a top-level ("Tier 1") supplier for the major auto companies, announced a joint venture with battery-maker Saft to produce and sell NiMH and Li-ion batteries for hybrids and electric vehicles. In March 2006, Boshart Engineering and Altair Nanotechnologies Inc. announced a joint venture to design an electric vehicle using Altair's Li-ion batteries. Boshart specializes in homologation services and has worked for major auto companies and their top-level suppliers.

A number of companies created the Advance Hybrid Vehicle Development Consortium. Raser Technologies, which makes electric motors, Electrovaya, which makes Li-ion batteries, Maxwell Technologies, which makes ultracapacitors, and Pacific Gas and Electric utility kicked it off, and other companies have joined in. Their goal: help compress a typical 15-year R&D cycle for a new vehicle down to 5 years or less for plug-in hybrids.

That can happen if the Consortium can help define the specifications and standards for plug-in hybrid vehicles and help drum up federal financial incentives so that automakers can sell the cars from the very start at prices that don't reflect the current cost of batteries, but their cost down the road once they're mass-produced. "It's called investing in price," says Raser Technologies' David West. "That's what the Japanese did [with hybrids]. They went large-market." It worked.

Another program already has put plug-in hybrids on the road. The Electric Power Research Institute (EPRI) hired Daimler-Chrysler to build and test prototype plug-in hybrid Sprinter panel vans, the kind used for commercial deliveries. Daimler-Chrysler first tested two of them in Stuttgart, Germany, then delivered two more to Los Angeles. Plans call for another two plug-in hybrid Sprinters to go to Kansas City and New York in 2006, and a total of 40 of the vans in the United States and Europe by the end of 2007. The two vans in Los Angeles went to Southern California Edison (with NiMH batteries) and the South Coast Air Quality Management District (with Li-ion batteries). Both have an electric range of 20 miles (32 km), use a gasoline engine as backup, and can carry a payload of at least 2,200 pounds (1,000 kg). The European versions use diesel engines instead of gasoline to support the electric drive.

The US Sprinter plug-in hybrids will be put through their paces by the likes of Federal Express, the New York Times, and other companies in the testing program. Initial testing in Stuttgart shows that the plug-in hybrid Sprinters reduce fuel use and CO_2 emissions by 10%–50% compared with a conventional diesel-powered Sprinter, depending on how the vehicles are driven. On average, the plug-in hybrid Sprinter gets about a 20% decrease in fuel use and greenhouse gas emissions, according to Daimler-Chrysler's Dominique Portmann.[3] Asked how much the price of Li-ion batteries needs to drop before they're commercially practical for plug-in hybrids, he said the price would need to drop by a factor of 10 between 2005 and 2010. "The way it's going, this is very well possible," Portmann said.

While everyone's waiting for the major automakers to make plug-in hybrids available, some are moving forward with the next-best thing — converting existing vehicles to plug-in hybrids. The City of Fresno, California, situated in the state's San Joaquin Valley cesspool of air pollution, has hired a New York company to make a plug-in series-hybrid trash truck for testing

on its stop-and-go routes. Hauppauge-based Odyne Corporation specializes in alternative-fuel heavy-duty trucks. The company is negotiating with other government agencies in New York
and California for possible conversions of plug-in para-transit
buses, light-transit buses, and more refuse trucks. Fresno officials
hope the plug-in hybrid trucks will help reduce the air pollution
that costs local residents and businesses $3 billion a year in asthma
attacks, premature deaths, lost work days, school absences, and
hospital admissions.[4]

A Canadian power company planned to launch a plug-in
hybrid trial program in 2006. "We are looking very seriously at
going to plug-in technology very quickly. I would think within
two or three years we'll have plug-in hybrid trucks," Manitoba
Hydro's Fleet Manager Ken Thomas said.[5] The utility's power-
planning division is greatly interested in the vehicle-to-grid
capabilities of plug-in hybrids, and he'd like the vehicles to reduce
the company fleet's gasoline use and emissions.

Manitoba Hydro will start by testing a plug-in hybrid service
truck and a converted plug-in hybrid Prius to gauge how well
they hold up in Canada's winter. "We figure, if it will work in
Winnipeg, it will work just about anywhere," Thomas says.

Another Canadian company announced that it soon would
offer Toyota Prius conversions to plug-in hybrids for governments and fleet owners, and possibly for consumers after that.
Toronto-based Hymotion said it also was working on a conversion kit for the flex-fuel Ford Escape SUV, which can run on
gasoline or E85 (85% ethanol blended with 15% gasoline). Like
EDrive, the company based in Monrovia, California, that hopes
to offer conversion services, Hymotion's kits feature Li-ion batteries.

EDrive's 9-kWh pack should give a Prius an electric range of
35 miles (56 km) and fuel efficiency of up to 150 miles (240 km)
per gallon. The conversion service will cost an expected $10,000–
$12,000. Hymotion's 5-kWh battery pack should give a Prius an
electric range of 31 miles (50 km) and efficiency of up to 100 miles
(160 km) per gallon. Hymotion hopes to sell the kits and installa-
tion for $9,500 per car for orders of more than 100 or $6,500 each

for orders of more than 1,000. By May 2006 there were 11 plug-in hybrid conversions on the road, 7 by EnergyCS with Li-ion batteries, 2 by CalCars with lead-acid batteries, 1 by Hymotion with Li-ion batteries, and 1 by Electro Energy with NiMH batteries.

Dozens of do-it-yourselfers took matters into their own hands by forming a special-interest group within the Electric Auto Association focused on plug-in hybrid conversions. Many of them already had converted gasoline cars to electric. They teamed up with Ron Gremban of the California Cars Initiative (Cal-Cars) to create schematics and a how-to guide for hobbyists to help them do their own plug-in hybrid conversions, and made it all open-source on the Web. For Earth Day 2006, CalCars staged a public conversion of a Prius to a PRIUS+ at a fair sponsored by *Make* magazine, called the Maker Faire, in San Mateo, California.

Automakers that initially ignored hybrids, including Volkswagen, Audi, and Porsche, have joined the hybrid bandwagon, positioning them to make future plug-in hybrids. Hyundai announced in September of 2005 that it would shift its focus from hydrogen fuel-cell research to hybrids.

The US Department of Energy held its first Plug-in Hybrid Electric Vehicle Discussion Meeting in May 2006, an invitation-only gathering of 150 representatives from seven automakers, industry suppliers, federal agencies and research labs, energy companies, activist organizations, and others. The same month, the association of shareholder-owned electric companies, Edison Electric Institute, followed the lead of publicly owned power companies and endorsed plug-in hybrids.

A comeback for all-electric vehicles began to seem possible, too. In June 2006 Fuji Heavy Industries (which makes Subarus) and the Tokyo Electric Power Company unveiled the R1e minicar, with a top speed of 62mph (100 km/h), a range of about 100 miles (80 km), and the ability to recharge to 80% of capacity in 15 minutes. If tests of the first 40 go well, the utility will place 500 per year in its fleet, and commercial sales could start by 2009.

GREENS

More and more high-profile environmentalists began plugging plug-in hybrids. Robert F. Kennedy, Jr., senior attorney for the Natural Resources Defense Council (NRDC), said, "We should have a national program to promote plug-in hybrid cars running on electricity and biofuels." The NRDC's vehicles campaign director, Deron Lovaas, published editorials in newspapers across the country, co-authored by the Institute for the Analysis of Global Security's Gail Luft, urging the United States to move en masse toward plug-in hybrids. Author and entrepreneur Paul Hawken twice lauded plug-in hybrids during a speech at the headquarters of Internet giant Google.

The media had a field day in early 2006 when it discovered that the Bush administration had been editing out evidence of global warming from National Aeronautic and Space Administration (NASA) reports and trying to prevent James E. Hansen, PhD, from speaking to the media. Hansen, NASA's top climate expert and director of its Goddard Institute for Space Studies at Columbia University, NY, refused to be muzzled. He also drew attention to plug-in hybrids: "Vehicle emissions are the greatest challenge that we must overcome to stabilize climate. The plug-in hybrid approach, as being pursued by CalCars, seems to be our best bet for controlling vehicle CO_2 emissions in the near term."

In one radio interview, Hansen described giving a talk at ExxonMobil headquarters to a group of executives from all the major automobile manufacturers and explaining to them the coming climate crisis caused by emissions: "I suggested, 'Why don't you try to get ahead of the curve and start emphasizing high-efficiency automobiles and get ahead of other manufacturers in the rest of the world?' The answer was, 'Dr. Hansen, we have to give the consumers what they want. And the consumers want bigger vehicles, more power, higher-performance vehicles. They don't want efficient automobiles.' They're going to have the ocean in their laps."[6]

Activists kept holding automakers' feet to the fire. The Jumpstart Ford campaign asked AutoNation, the largest US automotive retailer, to join the Plug-in Partners campaign and begin taking soft orders from the public for plug-in hybrids. Five members of Jumpstart Ford and the anti-war group Raging Grannies were arrested after blocking traffic by chaining themselves to mock oil barrels fastened to the gate of a Northern California Ford dealership.

Protesters from Plug In America outnumbered hydrogen boosters at the opening of a state-funded hydrogen fueling station in Burbank, California. The station, which cost almost $1 million, uses electricity to get hydrogen from natural gas in order to fuel six Prius hybrids that were modified to burn hydrogen instead of gasoline. It would be less expensive and less complicated to use the natural gas in cars that run on compressed natural gas, the activists pointed out. The amount of electricity needed to make enough hydrogen to drive the six cars a total of 600 miles (960 km) per day (100 miles or 160 km each) could have powered a fleet of 40–75 RAV4-EVs for 3,000 miles (4,800 km).

In May 2006 Chelsea Sexton lunched with a GM insider who told her that all the protests, publicity, and persistent calls for plug-in cars were moving both GM and Toyota to change direction. During the EV1 vigil, GM officials dismissed the protesters as "cute," but the sustained attention and mounting pressures were having an effect, her source said. Asked by a *Motor Trend* reporter about the company's worst mistakes, GM CEO Rick Wagoner replied, "Axing the EV1 electric-car program and not putting the right resources into hybrids. It didn't affect profitability, but it did affect image."[7]

Release of the documentary *Who Killed the Electric Car?* to critical acclaim in late June 2006 kept GM's black eye shining. Plug In America activists turned out at theaters to distribute flyers saying electric vehicles were "Not Dead Yet" and urging movie-goers to demand plug-in hybrids and electric cars. Two weeks before the film's debut, the sole EV1 on display in the Smithsonian Institution's National Museum of American History in Washington, DC, was removed from public view and replaced with a souped-up SUV. GM was the largest benefactor of the transportation exhibition hall, having donated $10 million in 2001 to pay for half its cost. The museum and the automaker denied any link between the film's release and the car's removal. The story spread widely in the media.[8]

Religious turf battles over the environmental moral high ground included car choices. Competing factions of evangelical Christians publicly issued dueling letters in February of 2006 about the need for creation care. First came a letter stating that "Bible-believing evangelicals…disagree about the cause, severity, and solutions to the global warming issue," signed by 22 high-profile evangelical leaders including James C. Dobson of Focus on the Family, Charles W. Colson of Prison Fellowship Ministries, Donald E. Wildmon of the American Family Association, and the Rev. Louis P. Sheldon of the Traditional Values Coalition.

A week later, 86 evangelical Christian leaders countered with a letter stating that global warming is real, it is human-induced, and its consequences especially affect the poor. They called for federal legislation to require reductions in greenhouse gas emissions through "cost-effective, market-based mechanisms." Signers included the presidents of 39 evangelical colleges, the head of the Salvation Army, well-known "megachurch" pastors such as Rick Warren, and prominent Black and Hispanic evangelical leaders. The letter was the first stage of an "Evangelical Climate Initiative" that planned to conduct educational campaigns in churches and colleges and to run TV and radio advertisements in nine states about the moral duty to stop global warming.[9]

Christians weren't the only ones feeling the moral imperative. Jewish, Roman Catholic, and Eastern Orthodox leaders also had climate campaigns brewing. Interfaith organizations in 15 states were lobbying for regional regulations to limit greenhouse gas emissions.

Due to the disagreement between members of the National Association of Evangelicals, NAE officials including Richard Cizik did not sign on to the global warming initiative, though he recruited others to sign the statement. A Prius driver, he believes plug-in hybrids could play an important role in creation care. "My vision is to see the evangelicals lead on the issue of hybrids now and plug-in hybrids when they're available," he said. "In fact, the 50 million evangelicals in this country ought to say to the car companies, 'We want your technology on the street as fast as possible.'"

OIL

Woolsey pitched plug-in hybrids everywhere he was invited. He appeared on cable TV's Comedy Central channel, explaining on *The Colbert Report* how flex-fuel plug-in hybrids could help keep dollars out of terrorists' bank accounts. He traveled again to California to give the keynote address at the annual conference of WestStart, a non-profit that supports public and private programs to develop cleaner vehicles. He testified alongside Amory Lovins of the Rocky Mountain Institute and others at a hearing on "US Energy Independence" held by the US Senate Committee on Energy and Natural Resources.

Concern about the coming competition for declining oil reserves was a theme being heard around the world. Finance ministers from the Group of Eight industrialized nations warned in February 2006 that "high and volatile energy prices" threaten global economic growth. They called for greater efforts to stabilize worldwide energy supplies.[10]

Sweden became the first country to set a goal of freeing its industry and economy from dependence on oil by 2020. A joint program between the Swedish government and GM displayed a plug-in parallel-hybrid Saab convertible at the Stockholm Auto Show in April 2006 that runs on electricity and 100% ethanol. The automakers touted it as the first fossil-fuel-free hybrid, but they hid the plug from the public. Just days before the show, GM ordered its Saab division to rewrite the press release on the 9-3 Convertible Biopower Hybrid Concept car to remove mention of its plug-in capability, and to glue shut the Saab emblem on the trunk that covers the electrical socket, a Swedish newspaper reported.[11] (I happened to print the original press release before all the online versions were edited.)

Securing America's Future Energy held another Oil Shockwave "war game," this time at the World Economic Forum's annual meeting in Davos, Switzerland, as part of a closed-door session with government and business leaders.

Real attacks — not make-believe — in Nigeria and Saudi Arabia in early 2006 threatened to disrupt world oil supplies. Nigerian militants already had knocked 445,000 barrels of oil per day out of the country's normal exports of 2.5 million barrels per day through attacks on pipelines and oil facilities. They pledged to step up attacks on oil facilities to cut daily exports by 1 million barrels.[12]

In Saudi Arabia, suicide bombers launched the first attack on the country's oil infrastructure, targeting the heavily fortified Abqaiq oil production center, responsible for about 10% of the world's daily oil production. Guards fired on two explosive-laden cars being driven by the terrorists, detonating them at a security gate about a mile from the main entrance. World markets jumped at the news, spiking oil prices by more than $1.20 per barrel, sending them above $62 a barrel.[13] By July 2006, oil cost $77 per barrel.

A corroded pipeline leaked more than 265,000 gallons of oil in northern Alaska in one of the worst spills in the 29-year history of the Trans-Alaska Pipeline, state Department of Environmental Conservation officials reported in March of 2006. A second leak was detected a week later. The leaks in the North Slope complex, located 300 miles (480 km) north of the Arctic Circle, spilled oil in a caribou crossing area of Prudhoe Bay.[14]

Military analysts sounded alarm bells about the end of the cheap oil era and how it threatens the military's ability to do its job. They urged a massive and immediate federal commitment to expand renewable energy installations.

"The railroads of the 19th century were built with massive government assistance in the form of loans, land grants, and other subsidies. In the 1950s, no one waited for the private sector to step in and provide a highway system. Modern computers, the Internet, and space technology all benefited immeasurably from government research, and indeed may have been inconceivable without government efforts," Nader Elhefnawy wrote in the magazine of the US Army War College.[15]

Since 1961 $40 billion in federal funding for research and development went to nuclear energy programs, $20 billion went to the fossil-fuel industry, and $10 billion was spent on renewable energy programs. "The progress of sources like wind and solar energy since the 1970s occurred not because of but in spite of the policies of the last quarter-century," Elhefnawy wrote.

A report by US Army Corps of Engineers analysts reached many of the same conclusions but was kept out of the public eye until a formal request for release was made by Rep. Roscoe Bartlett, a Maryland Republican who has taken the threat of peak oil to heart. The Army engineers warned that "the days of inexpensive, convenient, abundant energy sources are quickly drawing to a close." Oil and natural gas will become scarce and costly, coal is too dirty, and even the world's supply of low-cost uranium for nuclear power will be gone in about 20 years with current patterns of use, the report said.[16]

"Our best option for meeting future energy requirements are energy efficiency and renewable sources," the authors advised. "These options are available, sustainable, and secure. The affordability of renewable technologies is improving steadily and if the market is pulled by large Army application the cost reductions could be dramatic. For efficiency and renewables, the intangible and hard to quantify benefits — such as reduced pollution and increased security — yield indisputable economic value."

POLITICS

"America is addicted to oil."

With those words, President Bush had Americans cleaning out their earwax during his 2006 State of the Union speech, hardly believing what they'd heard. The neoconservatives who'd been pushing for plug-in hybrids weren't surprised, though. They'd been lobbying the administration for more than a year, and finally were seeing results.

Bush called for an "Advanced Energy Initiative" that would reduce US oil purchases by three-fourths of the amount imported from the Middle East by 2025. It also would provide $31 million for research on flexible-fuel and plug-in hybrid vehicles, among other strategies. His oil target would mean a decrease of only 4.5 million barrels of oil a day while the United States continued consuming 23 million barrels a day, and funding for research

California Cars Initiative (CalCars).

The first PRIUS+ in Ron Gremban's garage, as it appeared on the White House Website.

wouldn't move plug-in hybrids much closer to market. But coming from probably the biggest oil-boosting administration in US history, his speech was a sea change, Woolsey and other conservatives felt.

"It's the first step in a 12-step program," said Set America Free's Anne Korin.

On the White House website the day after Bush's address, Felix Kramer was surprised to see a familiar photo. There was the PRIUS+ peaking out of the tight confines of Ron Gremban's garage, with its CalCars bumper stickers and the license plate reading GAS OPT.

Bush didn't stop with one speech. Over the next month, he granted interviews to major media and toured the country promoting his energy initiative. In Colorado he visited solar-energy company United Solar Ovonic LLC and its founder, Stanford Ovshinsky, inventor of the NiMH battery. He spoke at a dinner for Republican stalwarts in Florida.

"I know it came as a shock to some to hear a Texan stand up there in front of the country and say, 'We've got a real problem.

America is addicted to oil.' But I meant it, because it's a true fact, and we've got to do something about it now," Bush said at every opportunity. In a speech at battery-maker Johnson Controls in Milwaukee, he added, "Our nation is on the threshold of some new energy technologies that I think will startle the American people. It's not going to startle you here at Johnson Controls because you know what I'm talking about."[17] In his simple, folksy fashion, he schooled listeners about plug-in hybrids: "Start picturing what I'm talking about. You've got your car, you pull in, you plug it right in the wall."

The US Conference of Mayors unanimously endorsed plug-in hybrids and urged automakers to manufacture them. New York Governor George Pataki proposed spending $44 million to make the state a leader in flex-fuel and plug-in hybrid development. Minnesota became the first state to pass legislation promoting plug-in hybrids, with universal backing from legislators and the governor, and the first state to place pre-orders with Austin's Plug-in Partners program. On the federal level, many Congressional leaders included plug-in hybrids in their plans. The bipartisan bills for the Fuel Choices for American Security Act were making their ways through the channels of the US Senate and House of Representatives. Another Senate bill proposed giving plug-in hybrids and vehicles that run on electricity or natural gas the same tax benefits already available to businesses that buy gasoline SUVs. The Environmental and Energy Study Institute featured Austin's Roger Duncan and EPRI's Bob Graham, among others, in a Congressional briefing on the potential for flex-fuel plug-in hybrids to reduce US dependence on oil, decrease greenhouse gases and other emissions, revitalize local economies, and lower fuel costs.

Brian Wynne of the Washington, DC-based Electric Drive Transportation Association described the momentum: "You can't swing a dead cat right now in this town and not hit a plug-in hybrid expert."

Few people in the US capitol had ever seen a plug-in hybrid, however, until CalCars and Set America Free arranged a grand introduction to coincide with testimony at a House Science

Subcommittee hearing in May 2006. Electro Energy drove its plug-in Prius with NiMH batteries to the capitol from Connecticut. Felix Kramer was able to show off his Prius, recently converted to a plug-in with Li-ion batteries by EnergyCS, by flying it from California to Washington. He raised $25,000 in one week through online appeals to CalCars supporters, explaining that other commitments for the car left no time to drive it or ship it across country by ground. After Kramer, Andrew Frank, and Austin's Roger Duncan spoke before the subcommittee, 24 senators and representatives and lots of their staff turned out for photo ops and rides in the cars with Jim Woolsey, Anne Korin, Frank Gaffney, and others.[18]

When Japan's Prime Minister Junichiro Koizumi told the press that his country should produce electric cars to reduce its reliance on imported oil and to protect the environment, Plug In America's Marc Geller wrote to him about the excellent performance of Toyota's RAV4-EVs in California, and about Toyota's thwarted efforts to destroy them. A representative of the Japanese Consulate called Geller for a long chat and then arranged a meeting with Ed Kjaer to visit Southern California Edison's fleet of RAV4-EVs.

Oil continued to make certain international relations difficult for the United States. Iran threatened to interrupt oil exports if the International Atomic Energy Agency took the issue of Iran's nuclear program to the United Nations Security Council. The United States threatened to hurt Iran if it cut off oil supplies.[19] When the issue did go to the Security Council, China and Russia vetoed the attempt to get a statement demanding that Iran clear up suspicions about its nuclear program.[20] Because of China's growing need for oil, Iran essentially has bought itself a seat on the Security Council, some analysts believe.

President Bush made a visit to the other rising competitor for global oil, India, in late February of 2006. There he proposed a deal to help India develop its civilian nuclear industry, but the subtext was oil. The more India switched to nuclear power, the less it might need oil for its growing economy, and the more oil might be available to the United States. The proposal caught flak back in the United States, where Bush also had been talking up the prospects for more nuclear plants.

All of his speeches promoting flex-fuel and plug-in hybrid vehicles didn't just include those options. Ranking alongside them in his list of solutions to America's oil addiction were calls to increase drilling for oil and natural gas on protected federal lands, greater use of coal, and construction of 19 new nuclear power plants in the United States by the end of the decade. Higher Corporate Average Fuel Economy (CAFE) standards weren't on the list.

There's little hope for public consensus on most of these options. In the search for solutions to our oil dependence, common ground holds plug-in hybrids, and not much else.

CHAPTER 11

Bridging a Divided America

SOMETIMES IT SEEMS like there's very little that Americans agree on today. In each of the hot-button issues related to plug-in hybrids, there are plenty of topics generating conflict that have yet to be blessed by a whiff of consensus. Yet in each area, plug-in hybrids emerge as a point of agreement, a beacon that can guide us out of our ideological stalemates and help us move toward a safer and more sustainable society.

THE END OF CHEAP OIL

Whether you believe that world oil production already has peaked or that it won't peak until 2030, it's obvious that increasing demand from China, India, and other growing economies plus the inevitably declining oil reserves mean that the era of inexpensive oil is over. The sooner we begin to move away from oil, the better.

It's also become painfully obvious that political, religious, social, and military conflicts within (and with) the countries that control most of the world's oil decrease the national security of both countries that rely on oil and countries that have the oil. By July of 2006, the US war in Iraq had killed 2,500 US soldiers, wounded 18,000 more, and cost the US close to $400 billion, not to mention untold thousands of Iraqi casualties.

The fact that US transportation depends almost exclusively on one type of fuel — petroleum — gives terrorists an easy target to inflict harm on the US economy.

We've got two options: increase supplies of oil, and decrease our need for it.

The option of opening up environmentally sensitive lands such as the Arctic National Wildlife Refuge to oil and gas drilling is a political stalemate, and not much of a solution anyway. The fossil fuels obtained would feed America's oil addiction for only a brief blip in time, while wreaking long-lasting environmental damage.

A lot of attention is being paid to getting petroleum from "unconventional" sources — a euphemism for dirtier, more difficult, and more costly sources. These highlight the desperate measures we're taking to continue with our oil-based society as long as possible. Drilling in ever-deeper ocean wells is a risky and temporary fix. The process of squeezing oil out of the tar sands of Canada ravages the lands, is relatively inefficient, and releases three times as much greenhouse gases as does producing conventional oil.

Rather than trying continuously to increase oil supplies, it will be less disruptive, safer, and easier to decrease our demand for fossil fuels. Plug-in hybrids offer the quickest way to free US transportation from oil and gasoline. After the Arab oil embargo of the 1970s, the United States revamped its electrical grid in roughly a decade to nearly eliminate oil as a source for electricity. The country could get its transportation system nearly off oil over the coming decade, if it has the will.

GLOBAL WARMING

The earth is warming, and humans are pumping an unhealthy burden of greenhouse gases into the atmosphere. The vast majority of credible scientists link those two trends and predict some dire consequences if these continue. Attempts to cast doubt on humans' role in global warming usually get exposed as diversionary tactics by companies or politicians who are comfortable with the status quo and who don't want to face the tougher question of what to do about the problem.

Since 33%–40% of US greenhouse gas emissions come from cars and light trucks, we've got to clean up car exhaust. The simplest and most long-sought solution is to improve the fuel efficiency of conventional cars through higher Corporate Average Fuel Economy (CAFE) standards, but as long as vehicles keep relying solely on gasoline, they're not going to be clean enough.

Besides, the quest for tougher CAFE standards is another political stalemate. Woolsey likens it to World War I, with both sides (the car companies and the environmentalists) hunkered down in their trenches, endlessly taking potshots at each other. I think that's understating the automakers' advantage. It's more like a medieval siege, with the car companies safely ensconced in their castle, surrounded by a protective moat of cash-hungry politicians, and with plenty of provisions to outlast the distant throngs of environmentalists, whose arrows bounce off the fortress walls.

Plug-in hybrids have emerged as another route into the castle, without having to deal with CAFE standards. While environmentalists have been seeking a standard of 40 miles (64 km) per gallon in the light-vehicle fleet, plug-in hybrids give us 100 miles (160 km) per gallon, and much more if they're flex-fuel plug-in hybrids.

Which isn't to say that we don't need better CAFE standards. We do, since automakers will be churning out millions more gasoline vehicles before plug-in hybrids comprise a significant share of the market. We should be wary of abandoning the quest for CAFE improvements as part of any deal with the auto industry to produce new-technology vehicles, given the sorry record of that strategy in the 1990s Partnership for a New Generation of Vehicles. And now that there are two powerful motivators for higher efficiency — independence from oil, and reduced emissions — perhaps the chances to boost CAFE standards have improved.

Plug-in hybrids and CAFE standards are not either-or propositions. With little time left to start setting our climate right before facing irreversible global-warming problems, it makes sense to put at least as much effort, if not more, into promoting plug-in hybrids as into lobbying for higher CAFE standards.

Car company representatives suddenly become concerned about the environment when talk turns to plug-in cars, claiming that emissions from power plants will create more greenhouse gases than plug-in cars eliminate. Their sentiment would be touching if it wasn't so hypocritical and inaccurate. I asked Toyota and Ford representatives multiple times to produce *any* evidence that plug-in vehicles would be worse for global warming than hybrids or gasoline vehicles, and neither company had anything to show.

In my research of studies on well-to-wheels emissions, I found only one scenario in a minority of studies in which this might be the case: if the power for all-electric cars comes from nothing but coal, and the electric cars are compared with hybrids. But car companies aren't going to sell their products only in the few states that get a high percentage of their power from coal. In the United States as a whole, using the 2005 mixture of power plants (50% coal, 19% nuclear, 19% natural gas, 6% hydroelectric, 3% petroleum, and 3% renewable), switching from gasoline to either electric or plug-in hybrid vehicles would produce less greenhouse gas emissions, multiple studies show. If we ensure that the grid keeps getting cleaner over time, plug-in cars will get even cleaner. More than 120 new coal-fired power plants have been proposed in the United States, however, so advocates for clean power and clean vehicles must work hand in hand to limit dirty forms of electricity and demand clean renewable power.

Just as federal regulations limit smog-forming pollutants from tailpipes and power plants, laws capping carbon emissions are needed to drive society's migration to cleaner cars and power plants. Advocates of plug-in hybrids and of renewable energy are natural allies on this issue. Once carbon is capped, the bogus issue of plug-in cars producing more well-to-wheels greenhouse gases goes away for good.

ALTERNATIVE ENERGY

If we're to power more of society by electricity, it makes sense to pay attention to the sources of electricity. Renewable wind and solar power hold the closest thing to consensus in the question of ideal sources of electricity. Almost everyone agrees that wind and solar power are a good thing. The question is, will they be enough of a good thing to meet our energy demands?

Plug-in vehicles help answer that question in two ways. One is through their emphasis on energy efficiency. Energy experts estimate that present US electricity consumption could be reduced 24% through energy-efficiency measures. We've had the luxury of largely ignoring energy efficiency, but fossil fuel constraints and climate constraints should put efficiency front and center in future energy policies. Electric vehicles indisputably are the most efficient motor vehicles.

Plug-in hybrids also provide a solution to one of the weaknesses of solar and wind — their intermittent production. If the power that's produced doesn't get used immediately, it needs to be stored somewhere. Plug-in vehicle batteries, which get charged mainly at night, work especially well to store wind power, which blows mainly at night. And vehicle-to-grid technology, which can move that stored energy from batteries back to the grid, makes wind power available whenever we need it most. Parking garages or carports equipped with solar panels can feed daytime electricity to parked cars away from home for vehicle-to-grid opportunities too.

Other energy alternatives to oil are much more problematic. Natural gas comes from many of the same countries that we depend on for oil, and supplies will be declining, putting our national security at risk if we depend on gas. Coal is domestic and plentiful but extremely polluting. The idea of "cleaner coal" plants through carbon sequestration (injecting the greenhouse gases produced by coal underground) is a potentially dangerous and unproven proposal. Even a tiny leakage of CO_2 could contribute to global warming.

The idea of nuclear power is back in vogue, but should be a non-starter as long as there is no way to deal safely with nuclear waste (which there isn't). World demand for uranium will exceed supply by 2015, according to the World Nuclear Association. Nuclear plants are logical targets for terrorists. As Woolsey points out, safe energy is distributed energy. Nuclear power is the ultimate centralized mistake.

ALTERNATIVE FUELS

Electricity can't replace oil in every circumstance. Liquid or other types of fuels still will be needed in airplanes and other situations. Liquid fuels also are desirable to extend the range of electric vehicles in the form of plug-in hybrids. Should these fuels be gasoline? Diesel? Biodiesel? Ethanol? Liquid fuel made from coal? Even, perhaps someday, hydrogen? There are pros and cons to each, which I must leave to other books to explore.

Plug-in hybrids can work with any of these, and by greatly reducing the amount of fuel needed, plug-in hybrids make these fuels more available for other uses. For example, the US presently produces approximately 4 billion gallons of ethanol per year. It would need 140 billion gallons per year if all cars ran strictly on ethanol, but an estimated 40 billion gallons would suffice if the cars were plug-in hybrids. Biofuels can work well with plug-in hybrids, but in the short term they also may be competitors to plug-in hybrids. Automakers and the corn and soy bean industries are pouring huge amounts of money and political clout into promoting flex-fuel vehicles that could replace hydrogen fuel-cell cars as the latest distraction that delays introduction of plug-in hybrids and electric vehicles.

PRODUCT VIABILITY

Car companies don't say they can't make plug-in hybrids. They claim that the batteries aren't good enough, or that plug-in hybrids will be too expensive, and that consumers don't want them. As we've seen in the story of plug-in hybrids, none of these excuses hold water.

The US Department of Energy (DOE) declared nickel-metal hydride (NiMH) batteries to be "mature" technology nearly seven years ago, and already has declared at least one type of lithium-ion (Li-ion) battery to be mature. Existing batteries already can power plug-in hybrids, DOE researchers acknowledge, and they're now helping to define the optimal battery configuration. Since President Bush's declaration that America is addicted to oil, the DOE has been testing potential plug-in hybrid batteries and planned to release standards for performance and evaluation of batteries for plug-in hybrids by the fall of 2006. Don Hillebrand, director of Argonne National Laboratory's Center for Transportation Research, said plug-in hybrids could be ready for mass production in 2008.[1]

Finally driving his own plug-in Prius, converted with Li-ion batteries by EnergyCS, Felix Kramer happily reported on a typical day of driving in May 2006. After 51 miles of driving, most of that on highways, he averaged 124 miles (198 km) per gallon plus 123 Wh/mile of electricity. He used 39% of the gasoline he would have used in a regular Prius and reduced greenhouse gas emissions by nearly two thirds. It cost him $1.76 and would have cost $3.17 in his Prius before it became a plug-in, assuming gasoline cost $3 per gallon and electricity cost $0.08.5 per kWh.

Hundreds of NiMH-powered electric vehicles still on the road in California have driven millions of trouble-free, emission-free miles. The Daimler-Chrysler plug-in hybrid Sprinter vans and the growing number of conversions from hybrids to plug-in hybrids demonstrate that both NiMH and Li-ion batteries can do the job. Studies by the Electric Power Research Institute (EPRI) and others report that NiMH batteries can handle plug-in hybrids.

Cobasys, the company that controls the patents for most NiMH batteries, may or may not be willing to make them for plug-in hybrids or electric vehicles. Only a major automaker can call the company's bluff or purchase a large amount of batteries.

The mass production of hybrids has lowered the cost of plug-in hybrid components other than the batteries, and battery costs will fall with mass production. The high battery prices that automakers cite for hybrids don't apply to plug-in hybrids. So-called power batteries used in hybrids are more expensive than "energy" batteries used in electric vehicles (even when they're made with the same chemistry, like NiMH). Plug-in hybrid batteries fall somewhere in-between.

CONSUMER READINESS

Studies by the DOE and EPRI show that consumers will buy plug-in hybrids. The DOE's National Renewable Energy Laboratory hired Opinion Research Corporation International to survey 1,012 people in 2005. Even if gasoline cost a mere $1.50 per gallon, 36% of those who planned to buy a new vehicle within the next three years said that they would pay an extra $2,500 for a hybrid if it reduced gasoline use by 30%, and 15% said they would pay another $1,500 beyond that for a plug-in hybrid if it reduced gasoline use by 45% compared with a conventional vehicle.[2] If 15% of car buyers chose plug-in hybrids, eventually that would put 37 million plug-in hybrids on the road.

Similarly, research by EPRI's Hybrid Electric Vehicle Working Group (which included automakers) concluded that consumers would be willing to pay an extra $1,400 above the cost of a hybrid for a plug-in hybrid that has a 20-mile electric range.[3] EPRI plans to take another look at consumer acceptance of plug-in hybrids soon. Their original conclusions predated the terrorist attacks of September 11, 2001, the rising price of gasoline, the extended US war in Iraq, and the increased awareness of global warming.

A barrage of surveys reported growing consumer interest in fuel-efficient vehicles in 2006. In one poll by Harris Interactive, Inc., 80% of respondents said that fuel efficiency would affect their next purchase of a new car.[4] A survey of 500 households in April 2006 by Opinion Research Corp. showed that 75% of respondents had heard of plug-in hybrids, 55% thought they were a good idea, and 75% park in a driveway, carport, or garage, presumably near an electrical outlet, reported Ed Wall of the US Department of Energy's Office of FreedomCAR and Vehicle Technologies. An online survey that month by *The Wall Street Journal* and pollsters Harris Interactive found that 33% of 2,516 US adults who plan to purchase or lease a new vehicle are most likely to seriously consider an alternative-fuel vehicle, mainly due to concerns about the environment and fuel costs. Of these, 92% are willing to pay an average $9,258 extra for the vehicle.[5] High gasoline prices have 37% of US consumers considering replacing their cars with more fuel-efficient versions, according to a May 2006 survey by *Consumer Reports*.[6]

The fierce devotion to electric vehicles by people who got a chance to drive them demonstrates the kind of loyalty that builds when people experience clean driving. And Plug-in Partners is building a new database of ready customers to plunk into the lap of any company willing to make a plug-in hybrid.

AUTOMAKERS' EVOLUTION

Several signs by mid-2006 suggested that plug-in hybrids are on the horizon. Toyota executive Shiniche Abe told *The Guardian* newspaper in April 2006 that the next version of the Prius in 2008 would be a plug-in hybrid with a nine-mile electric range.[7] After years of pooh-poohing the idea and claiming that plug-in hybrids and electric vehicles would increase pollution, Toyota spokeswoman Cindy Knight said in June 2006, "It is something we are seriously looking at. We think this kind of thing does have potential, under the right circumstances, to increase fuel economy and reduce CO_2 emissions."[8] Toyota North America Inc. President Jim Press confirmed in late July 2006 that the company plans to pursue a plug-in hybrid vehicle.[9]

Questioned by Jennifer Krill of Rainforest Action Network and other activists at the Ford shareholders meeting in May 2006, CEO Bill Ford said, "We are looking very keenly" at plug-in hybrids "and working with that technology." A month later, however, Ford announced it was backing away from plans to build 250,000 hybrids by 2010 and would pursue an array of alternative technologies. Ford's average vehicle fuel efficiency of 19.1mpg remained the lowest of all automakers.

Bloomberg News and CNNMoney.com ran separate stories on June 23, 2006 saying GM is developing a plug-in hybrid that will get more than 60mpg, citing unnamed sources inside the company. Publicly, GM spokespeople declined to comment, but they didn't deny it. The car may be shown at the Detroit Auto

Show in January 2007 and could be for sale a year later.[10] Another GM insider told EVWorld.com editor Bill Moore that GM not only was investigating plug-in hybrids but was taking another look at electric vehicles.

LOOKING AHEAD

Smart companies plan ahead and try to be the first to adopt new technology that will give them a competitive advantage. That's what Toyota and Honda did with hybrids, and now they're sitting pretty. Whichever company is first to bring a good plug-in hybrid to market will not only change their fortune but change the world.

Any number of things could stifle plug-in hybrid production, however, and — as we saw with the Zero-Emission Vehicle (ZEV) Mandate struggles — even getting plug-in hybrids to market doesn't mean they'll stay here. A temporary drop in gasoline prices, lawsuits by the car companies, misinformation campaigns by the oil companies, weakening of government regulations: All have quashed previous attempts to bring consumers alternative-fuel vehicle options.

A number of things are different this time around. The forces pushing us to get away from oil are greater than ever — global warming, national security, oil's threat to economic stability, and costs to consumers. We also have broader alliances collaborating with each other, some for the first time, to achieve common goals.

Politicians are crossing party-line barriers (something seldom seen in Washington) in bipartisan support for plug-in hybrids. Many constituencies have reason to work together for plug-in hybrids: scientists; environmentalists; national-security analysts, and advocates of biofuels, electric vehicles, and renewable energy.

Each one of us will play a role in the ending of this story.

WHAT CAN YOU DO?

- Make your actions an agent of change. Walk more. Ride a bike. Take mass transit. Less driving means less oil consumption and fewer greenhouse gas emissions.

- If you live in a large city, chances are there's a car-sharing organization that you can join instead of owning your own car, like City CarShare, ZipCar, or FlexCar. Ask your local car-share organization to join Austin's Plug-in Partners campaign (<www.pluginpartners.org>) and pledge to buy plug-in hybrids for their fleets.
- If you must have a vehicle, get an electric bike, electric scooter, or neighborhood electric vehicle instead of another gasoline vehicle. Choose a new plug-in hybrid or electric vehicle when they become available, or consider buying a used electric vehicle from classified ads posted at <www.evfinder.com>.
- Mitsubishi and Subaru have announced that they plan to sell new electric vehicles in 2008 and 2009, probably initially in Japan only. Ask them to sell electric vehicles and plug-in hybrids in North America. Call Subaru at 800-SUBARU3 and Mitsubishi at 714-372-6000.
- Contact other major automakers and tell them that you want the option of buying a plug-in hybrid or electric vehicle. Start by calling Toyota at 800-331-4331, Ford at 800-392-FORD, and GM/Saturn at 800-553-6000.
- Join Plug In America (<www.pluginamerica.com>) and stay abreast of the most recent actions to promote plug-in hybrids and electric vehicles.
- Sign the Plug-in Partners pledge (<www.pluginpartners .com>) saying that you'd like the option of buying a plug-in hybrid. Get your city, county, business, school district, college, house of worship, or organization to join Plug-in Partners. If they have a vehicle fleet of any size, ask them to place "soft orders" for future purchases of plug-in hybrids through Plug-in Partners.
- Work with your favorite environmental organization to boost support for plug-in hybrids.
- If you're concerned about national security, support Set America Free (<www.setamericafree.org>). Let your elected representatives know about Set America Free's support for plug-in hybrids.
- Call your favorite car dealer and say that you won't buy

another new car, truck, or SUV until they offer the option of a plug-in hybrid.

- If you own a Prius, consider converting it to a plug-in hybrid through EDrive or Hymotion once their consumer services are up and running.
- If you're a car tinkerer, consider converting a Prius (2004 or more recent models) to a plug-in hybrid yourself. Find out how through the Electric Auto Association's special interest group at <www.eaa-phev.org>.
- Be conscious of the energy that you use. Install efficient fluorescent light bulbs in your home, buy efficient appliances, and get solar panels when you can afford them.
- If you're an investor, put your money into companies that support plug-in hybrid technology.
- Urge the California Air Resources Board to tighten regulations so that automakers produce the plug-in hybrids and electric vehicles that we know they can make. Since other US states can choose between California standards and federal standards, the Board holds the key to cleaner cars throughout the country. E-mail helpline@carb.ca.gov, or call 1-800-242-4450, or write to California Air Resources Board, 1001 I Street, P.O. Box 2815, Sacramento, CA 95812.
- Perhaps most important, communicate with your elected representatives and with government officials to make sure that they create the incentives and the regulations — the carrots and the sticks — that will bring plug-in hybrids to market, and keep them here. Do this on local (city or county), state (or provincial), and national levels.

S. David Freeman, an energy official in the Carter Administration and now president of the Los Angeles Board of Harbor Commissioners, says it best in the documentary, *Who Killed the Electric Car?*:

The oil industry and the auto companies are resistant to change. The American people need to be reminded that it took a law to get seat belts in the cars. It took a law to get air bags in the cars. It took a law to get the mileage up from 12 to 20 miles per gallon.

It took a law to get catalytic converters to control the pollution. I think clean cars are too important to be left to the automobile industry.

In a democracy, it's up to us to make sure the politicians give us the laws and regulations that we need.

When the people of a divided country come together, and their plan is sound, wonderful things can happen. Each of us can help bring our country closer to the day when we live in a cleaner, safer society. Plug-in hybrids can help get us there.

Let's get rolling.

Acknowledgments

M Y THANKS GO OUT to many people who helped make this book possible, but first and foremost to Chris Plant of New Society Publishers for his vision and persistence in bringing it to life.

I am grateful for the counsel of those who reviewed all or parts of the manuscript: Barbara Baker; Red Bennett; Charles Garlow; Meg Newman; Jerry Pohorsky, and Noam Szoke.

People who were willing to be interviewed repeatedly for the book and to review excerpts deserve extra thanks: Andrew Frank; Marc Geller; Ron Gremban; Felix Kramer; Chelsea Sexton, and R. James Woolsey.

Others granted interviews or provided assistance and have my gratitude: James Barnes; Dave Barthmuss; Karen Bauer; Heather Bernikoff; Dean Case; Richard Cizik; Roger Duncan; Tien Duong; Tom Gage; Dave Goldstein; Truls Gulowsen; Greg Hanssen; Roland Hwang; Cindy Knight; Anne Korin; Jennifer Krill; Therese Langer; Gunnar Lindstrom; Kevin Lyons; Jason Mark (of Global Exchange); Jason Mark (of the Union of Concerned Scientists); Dave Modisette; Philip Patterson; Dave Raboy; Wally Rippel; Joseph Romm; Paul Scott; Ichiro Sugioka; Ken Thomas; Nick Twork; David West, and Michael Q. Wang.

Others who could not go on record still shared their insights and information from the automobile, electric utility, and battery industries, for which I am deeply grateful.

I am fortunate to be associated with organizations whose advocacy of electric vehicles and plug-in hybrids put me in a position to write this book: the San Francisco Electric Vehicles Association (sfeva.org); the Electric Auto Association (eaa-ev.org); Plug In America (pluginamerica.org), and the California Cars Initiative (calcars.org). A special shout-out goes to the thousands of people across the country who fought to bring electric vehicles to the market and to save them from destruction, or who have converted gasoline cars to electric vehicles or to plug-in hybrids to show it can be done.

Securing America's Future Energy was kind enough to provide a transcript of its Oil Shockwave and other materials. I'm grateful to the Electric Drive Transportation Association for allowing use of the diagrams in chapter 2 and for granting me a press pass to its annual conference. Thanks go to Meridian International Research for granting permission to use the chart in chapter 8, to the National Commission on Energy Policy for providing background materials, and to Terry Wilson, historian of the Electric Auto Association, for sharing his library.

I would have been unable to write this book without the leave of absence generously granted by my employer, International Medical News Group, a division of Elsevier, and the support of my chief editor there, Mary Jo Dales.

Finally, I have been sustained for the past 23 years by the love and support of my life partner, Meg Newman, MD, whose shining example moves me to contribute what I can to the world. To the young people who inspire me to leave the earth in better shape for them to inherit — Red, Sean, Andrew, Eleanor, Margaret, and Maya — I send my love.

Notes

Chapter 1

1. Jim Motavalli, *Forward Drive: The Race to Build "Clean" Cars for the Future,* Sierra Club Books, 2000, p. 72.
2. Jim Klein and Martha Olson, *Taken for a Ride,* New Day Films, 1996. [film, video].
3. Jim Motavalli, *Forward Drive: The Race to Build "Clean" Cars for the Future,* Sierra Club Books, 2000, pp. 39–43.
4. Michael Schnayerson, *The Car That Could,* Random House, 1996.
5. A GM supervisor relayed the comment to the Specialists.
6. California Air Resources Board, "Fact Sheet: 2003 Zero Emission Vehicle Program Changes," March 18, 2004.
7. Chris Paine, *Who Killed the Electric Car?,* 90 minutes. Plinyminor and Dean Devlin's Electric Entertainment, 2006. [film].
8. Ibid.
9. Ibid.
10. Sources for Zero Emission Vehicle (ZEV) Timeline: California Air Resources Board (CARB) "Updated Informative Digest: Public Hearing to Consider Amendments to the California Zero-Emission Vehicle Regulations," 2001; CARB "Fact Sheet: 2003 Zero-Emission Vehicle Program Changes," 2004; Michael Schnayerson, *The Car that Could,* Random House, 2006; Jim Motavalli, *Forward Drive,* Sierra Club Books, 2000; Thomas J. Knipe et al, "100,000-Mile Evaluation of the Toyota RAV4 EV," Southern California Edison, 2002; Robert Collier, "Canada, carmakers sign tough emis-

sions pact," *San Francisco Chronicle,* April 6, 2005, A6; William McCall, "Ore. OKs Temporary Vehicle Emission Rules," The Associated Press, December 22, 2005; Kimberly Rogers, "Where are the Zero-Emission Vehicles?" <www.dare lldd.com/ev/carb_ruling.htm>; Mike Kane, "ZEV timeline," <www.darelldd.com/ev/dead_zev.htm>; Sierra Research, <www.sierraresearch.com/CVSNewsPrev1990.htm> and subsequent pages through 2006.

Chapter 2

1. National Commission on Energy Policy Technical Appendix, Chapter 6: Developing Better Energy Technologies for the Future, pp. 11–12.
2. Jim Motavalli, *Forward Drive,* Sierra Club Books, 2000, pp. 71–72.
3. Norihiko Shirouzu and Jathon Sapsford, "Power Struggle: As Hybrid Cars Gain Traction, Industry Battles Over Designs," *The Wall Street Journal,* October 19, 2005, A1.
4. "Average Dealership Profile," *AutoExec Magazine,* May 2005, p. 43.
5. "Tell Me More About Electricity! Electric Vehicles," Sacramento Municipal Utility District, <www.smud.org/safety/world/science/vehicles.html>.
6. "Full Fuel Cycle Emissions Reductions through the replacement of ICEVs with BEVs," prepared by the Electric Vehicle Association of Canada for Health Canada's Air and Waste Section, July 10, 2000.
7. M. Q. Wang, 2001, "GREET v. 1.6 Beta Fuel Use and Emissions Model," (computer spreadsheet) Argonne National Laboratory, Center for Transportation Research. Report ANL/ESD/TM-163.
8. "Plugging in to the Next Stage in HEV Technology," US Department of Energy Clean Cities Program, *Clean Cities Now,* 10(1), February 15, 2006, <www.eere.energy.gov/clean cities/ccn/progs/story.cgi/WHATS_NEW/530/0/A>
9. Greg Schneider, "Disparate Groups Agree on Need for Alternative to Oil Dependency," *Washington Post,* April 1, 2005.

10. Sholnn Freeman, "Pickup Buyers Want Efficiency, Survey Says," *Washington Post,* November 17, 2005, D2.

11. Electric Auto Association, "High Gas Prices Got You Down? Drive Electric!" May, 2005, <www.eaaev.org>.

12. "Plugging in to the Next Stage in HEV Technology," US Department of Energy Clean Cities Program, *Clean Cities Now,* 10(1), Feb. 15, 2006, <www.eere.energy.gov/cleancities/ccn/progs/story.cgi/WHATS_NEW/530/0/A>

13. Bill Moore, "The Coming Energy Convergence," *EV World,* January 6,2006, <www.evworld.com/view.cfm/section=article 7storyid=949>.

14. US Department of Transportation, Bureau of Transportation Statistics and Federal Highway Administration, 2001 National Household Travel Survey data, CD-ROM, February 2004.

15. US Department of Transportation Nationwide Personal Transportation Survey, 1990.

16. Personal communication by Philip Patterson, US Department of Energy.

Chapter 3

1. Jack Doyle, *Taken for a Ride,* Four Walls Eight Windows, 2000, pp. 421–429.

2. Judy Anderson and Curtis D. Anderson, *Electric and Hybrid Cars,* McFarland & Company, 2005, p. 51.

3. Chris Paine, *Who Killed the Electric Car?,* 90 minutes. Plinyminor and Dean Devlin's Electric Entertainment, 2006. [film].

4. Joseph Romm, "Reviewing the Hydrogen Fuel and Freedom-CAR Initiatives," testimony before the House Science Committee, March 3, 2004.

5. Joseph J. Romm and Andrew A. Frank, "Hybrid Vehicles Gain Traction," *Scientific American,* April 2006, pp. 72–79.

6. Patrick Mazza and Roel Hammerschlag, "Carrying the Energy Future: Comparing Hydrogen and Electricity for Transmission, Storage and Transportation," Institute for Lifecycle Environmental Assessment June 2004.

7. Ibid.

8. Joseph Romm, "Reviewing the Hydrogen Fuel and Freedom-CAR Initiatives," testimony before the House Science Committee, March 3, 2004.
9. Richard A. Lovett, "Addicted to Oil: How Can US Fulfill Bush Pledge?" *National Geographic News,* February 14, 2006.
10. Bill Moore, "Is the Bloom off the Hydrogen Rose?" EV World blog, December 10, 2005.
11. "Point/Counterpoint," online debate; Joe Romm referenced 2003 study by Royal Dutch/Shell, <www.pbs.org/wgbh/nova/sciencenow/3210/01-point.html>.
12. Larry Burns, "Hydrogen Gas," Jonathan Fahey, Forbes.com, April 25, 2005, <www.forbes.co/forbes/2005/0425/078_print.html>.

Chapter 4

1. Ernest H. Wakefield, PhD, "History of the Electric Automobile," Society of Automotive Engineers, 1998, p. 22.
2. Ibid., pp. 43–44.
3. Ibid., pp. 45–46.
4. Ibid., p. 57.
5. Ernest H. Wakefield, PhD, "History of the Electric Automobile," Society of Automotive Engineers, 1998, pp. 82–83.
6. Meridian International Research, "2007: Solving Peak Oil," August 16, 2005, p. 35.
7. Peter Hendriksen et al., "Audi Duo Demonstration Project: Environmental Comparison and User Survey," presented at EVS-17, Montreal, Canada, October 2000.
8. Dean Taylor, Southern California Edison, "Plug-in HEV Incentives," PowerPoint presentation at American Public Power Association conference, Nov. 17, 2005.
9. Ernest H. Wakefield, PhD, "History of the Electric Automobile," Society of Automotive Engineers, 1998, pp. 144–150.
10. Keith Bradsher, "High and Mighty; SUVs: The World's Most Dangerous Vehicles and How They Got That Way," Public Affairs, 2002, p. 11-12.
11. Jack Doyle, *Taken for a Ride,* Four Walls Eight Windows, 2000, pp. 395–419.

12. Personal communication.
13. Peter Day, "The Electric Car," BBC Radio, February 10, 2006.
14. "Plugging into the Future," *The Economist*, June 10-16, 2006, Technology Quarterly section, pp. 30–32.
15. M. Duvall, "Advanced Batteries for Electric-Drive Vehicles," Electric Power Research Institute Report 1009299, May 2004. The HEV Working Group estimated that a plug-in hybrid with a 20-mile electric range would get 33,000–66,000 miles out of the batteries, and one with a 40-mile electric range would get up to 100,000 miles out of the batteries, and the rest of the 150,000 miles in the life of the car would come from hybrid gas-electric mode driving. A fully electric vehicle would get 130,000–150,000 electric miles on one NiMH pack.
16. Ed Kjaer, Southern California Edison, PowerPoint presentation at American Public Power Association Plug-in Hybrid Symposium, November 2005.
17. Robert Schoenberger, "Addiction Fighter: Plug-in Hybrids Could Ease Oil Dependence," *The Courier-Journal*, Louisville, KY, April 2, 2006.
18. Meridian International Research, "2007: Peak Oil. The Electric Vehicle Imperative," November 2, 2005.
19. Meridian International Research, "2007: Solving Peak Oil," August 16, 2005.
20. Michael Schnayerson, *The Car That Could*, Random House, 1996, p. 222.

Chapter 5
1. Chris Dixon, "Carmakers Pull Plug on Electric Vehicles," *New York Times*, March 28, 2004, <www.nytimes.com/2004/03/28/automobiles/28AUTO.html?ex=1081378197ei=17en=f4 2e293c07679081>.
2. Elizabeth Weise, "Th!nk Drivers Strive to Save Their Cars from the Crusher," *USA Today*, September 2, 2004, <www.usa today.com/tech/news/2004-09-02-thinkcar_x.htm>.
3. Ibid.

4. Bill Moore, "Nordic Survival," <www.evworld.com>, November 8, 2005.

5. Chris Dixon, "Carmakers Pull Plug on Electric Vehicles," *New York Times*, March 28, 2004.

Chapter 6

1. Lauran Neergaard, "Study: More CO_2 Now than Past 650k Years," Associated Press, November 24, 2005, <www.breitbart.com/news/2005/11/24/D8E33F2G3.html>.

2. Michael Janofsky, "6 EPA Ex-Chiefs Urge Bush to Limit Carbon Emissions," *New York Times*, in the *San Francisco Chronicle*, January 19, 2006, A4.

3. Stephen Heckeroth, "Choose a Car to Stabilize the Climate and Your Wallet," presented at California Public Utilities Commission meeting, San Francisco, February 23, 2005.

4. Roland Hwang, "Driving Out Pollution: The Benefits of Electric Vehicles," Union of Concerned Scientists, 1994; emissions figures reprinted in "A Critical Evaluation of Electric Vehicle Benefits," Todd Litman, Victoria Transport Policy Institute, November 28, 1999.

5. Michael Schnayerson, *The Car That Could*, Random House, 1996, p. 153. He also cites *Motor Trend*, October 1993.

6. Broward County Department of Planning and Environmental Protection, "The Future of Electric Transportation in Broward County, Florida," 1999.

7. David Friedman, "A New Road: The Technology and Potential of Hybrid Vehicles," Union of Concerned Scientists, 2003.

8. Antonia Herzog and Marika Tatsutani, "A Hydrogen Future? An Economic and Environmental Assessment of Hydrogen Production Pathways," Natural Resources Defense Council, November 2005.

9. The sources for this section include (not a complete list):

M.Q. Wang, Argonne National Laboratory, "Development and Use of GREET 1.6 Fuel-cycle Model for Transportation Fuels and Vehicle Technologies," June 2001. Author's note: In a phone interview, Dr. Wang acknowledged an artifact in one section of the GREET 1.6 analysis of electric vehicles, and suggested averaging the figures that were reported as having a 20% and 80% probability of being correct. I used the averages for this analysis.

Gilbert Masters, PhD, professor of civil and environmental engineering, Stanford University, CA.

Joseph Romm, Center for Energy and Climate Solutions, Washington, DC.

Therese Langer and Daniel Williams: "Greener Fleets: Fuel Economy Progress and Prospects," Report Number T024, American Council for an Energy-Efficient Economy, December 2002.

"Climate Change" (Staff Report: Initial Statement of Reasons for Proposed Rulemaking, Public Hearing To Consider Adoption of Regulations to Control Greenhouse Gas Emissions from Motor Vehicles), California Environmental Protection Agency Air Resources Board, August 6, 2004.

Daryl Slusher, Austin Energy, presentation to Electric Drive Transportation Association, December 8, 2005.

Mark Kapner, Austin Energy, presentation to Electric Auto Association, April, 2005.

Chip Gribben, "Debunking the Myth of EVs and Smokestacks," Electric Vehicle Association of Greater Washington, DC, circa 1997.

"Draft Technology and Cost Assessment for Proposed Regulations to Reduce Vehicle Climate Change Emissions Pursuant to Assembly Bill 1493," California Air Resources Board, April 1, 2004.

Stephen Heckeroth, "Choose a Car to Stabilize the Climate and Your Wallet," 2005.

Jon Leonard, TIAX LLC, "Update to 2002 AD Little LEV EV Market Assessment," October 25, 2005.

Mark Duvall, Electric Power Research Institute, "Plug-in Hybrids Electric Vehicles," presentation to American Public Power Association, November 2005.

William Glauz, Los Angeles Department of Water and Power, "A Vision of the Future," presentation to American Public Power Association, November 2005.

Electric Vehicle Association of Canada, "Full Fuel Cycle Emissions Reductions Through the Replacement of ICEVs with BEVs," prepared for Health Canada, Air and Waste Section, July 10, 2000.

Broward County Board of County Commissioners, "The Future of Electric Transportation in Broward County, Florida," Department of Planning and Environmental Protection, 1999.

Todd Litman, "A Critical Evaluation of Electric Vehicle Benefits," Victoria (BC) Transport Policy Institute, November 28, 1999.

10. Natural Resources Defense Council, "Growing Energy: How Biofuels Can Help End America's Oil Dependence," December 2004.

11. M.Q. Wang, "Development and Use of GREET 1.6 Fuel-cycle Model for Transportation Fuels and Vehicle Technologies," Argonne National Laboratory, June 2001.

12. Energy Information Agency, US Department of Energy, "Electric Power Annual 2004," DOE/EIA-0348, November 2005, Table 5.1, p. 34. <www.eia.doe.gov/cneaf/electricity/epa/epa_sum.htm>.

13. "Wind Farms Could Meet Energy Needs," CNN.com, July 15, 2005. <www.cnn.com/2005/TECH/science/07/15/wind.power/index.html>.

14. Lester R. Brown, "The Shortcut to Energy Independence: Hybrid Cars and Wind Power Offer a Winning Combination," *Ode Magazine*, June 2005, pp. 18–19. Excerpted from *Mother Earth News*, February-March 2005.

15. Steven E. Letendre, Richard Perez, and Christy Herig, "Solar Vehicles at Last?" *Solar Today Magazine*, May/June 2006, pp. 26–29.

16. David Goodstein, *Out of Gas: The End of the Age of Oil*, W.W. Norton, 2004, p. 40.

17. Michael Totten, "A Solar Proliferation Plan," *Solar Today Magazine*, July/August 2005, p. 10.

18. Steven E. Letendre and Willett Kemptom, "The V2G Concept: A New Model for Power?" *Public Utilities Fortnightly*, February 15, 2002, pp. 16–26.

19. Willett Kemptom and Jasna Tomic, "Vehicle-to-Grid Power Implementation: From Stabilizing the Grid to Supporting Large-scale Renewable Energy," Journal of Power Sources, 2005, 144, pp. 280–294.

20. Mark Clayton, "Electric Cars That Pay," *Christian Science Monitor*, July 29, 2004, <www.cxmonitor.com/2004/0729/p17 s02-stct-html>.

Chapter 7

1. Woolsey's title is fictitious. Although he served as director of the CIA, he has not been the US Homeland Security chief. He and a bipartisan panel of former high-level government officials who participated in the "executive committee" were role-playing as part of the first "Oil Shockwave" crisis simulation held June 23, 2005, in Washington, DC and sponsored by Securing America's Future Energy and the National Commission on Energy Policy. Participants were informed in advance of their roles but not about the events and situations they would encounter.

2. The events in this chapter did not happen. The scenarios were invented by a team of former oil industry executives, economics experts, and government officials including Rand Beers, a White House counterterrorism official under President George Bush who quit in 2003 to protest the Iraq War. The descriptions were part of the first "Oil Shockwave" crisis simulation held June 23, 2005, in Washington, DC and sponsored by Securing America's Future Energy and the National Commission on Energy Policy. Dialogue is taken from the event's transcript.

3. Robert Baer, *Sleeping with the Devil: How Washington Sold Our Soul for Saudi Crude*, Crown Publishing Group, 2003.

Chapter 8

1. Frank J. Gaffney, Jr., "Freedom in Security: A Naked Energy Gap," *The National Review Online*, March 29, 2005.

2. Kenneth S. Deffeyes, *Beyond Oil: The View from Hubbert's Peak*, Hill and Wang, 2005, pp. xi–xv.

3. Ibid.
4. Seattle Post-Intelligencer Editorial Board, "Energy Policy; A World With Less Oil," July 11, 2005, <http://seattlepi.nw source.com/opinion/231850)energyed.asp>.
5. Robert E. Uhrig, PhD, "Using Plug-in Hybrid Vehicles," The Bent of Tau Beta Pi, Spring 2005, pp. 13–19.
6. Energy Policy Act 2005, Section 1837: National Security Review of International Energy Requirements, US Department of Energy, February 2006.
7. Ibid.
8. David Goodstein, *Out of Gas; The End of the Age of Oil*, W.W. Norton, 2004, p. 15.
9. Joseph Romm and Charles Curtis, "Mideast Oil Forever?" *Atlantic Monthly*, April 1996, <www.theatlantic.com/issues/96apr/oil/oil.htm>.
10. Edward Epstein, "Gas-thirsty Cars Imperil US, Conservative Ex-Officials Warn," *San Francisco Chronicle*, April 7, 2005.
11. George P. Shultz and R. James Woolsey, "Oil and Security: A Committee on the Present Danger Policy Paper," <www.fight ingterror.org/pdfs/07S8-5-05.pdf>.

Chapter 9

1. Meridian International Research, "2007: Solving Peak Oil," August 16, 2005.
2. Keith Kloor, "The Holy & the Hawks," *Audubon: Currents*, September 2005, <http://magazine.audubon.org/currents/currents0509.html>.
3. Bob Graham, Electric Power Research Institute, presentation to Electric Drive Transporation Association, Vancouver, BC, December 8, 2005.

Chapter 10

1. Chris Paine, *Who Killed the Electric Car?*, 90 minutes. Plinyminor and Dean Devlin's Electric Entertainment, 2006, [film].
2. *New York Times* Editorial Board, "Trying to Find the Road Ahead," January 24, 2006, A24.

3. Dominique Portmann, DaimlerChrysler, presentation to Electric Drive Transportation Association, Vancouver, BC, December 8, 2005.

4. Greg Lucas, "Cost of Polluted Air in Billions, Study Says," *San Francisco Chronicle*, March 30, 2006, B3.

5. Bill Redekop, "Hydro to Test Plug-in Hybrids", *Winnipeg Free Press*, January 6, 2006.

6. Dr. Hansen interviewed on *On Point* with host Tom Ashbrook, WBUR Radio, Boston, February 2, 2006: <www.onpointradio.org/shows/2006/02/20060203_a_main.asp>.

7. Posting by John McGrath, "Well No Kidding," *Grist*, June 28, 2006. <http://gristmill.gristorg/story/2006/6/28/174247/184>.

8. Linda Hales, "An Electric Car, Booted," *The Washington Post*, June 16, 2006, C01.

9. Lauri Goodstein, "Evangelic Leaders Join Global Warming Initiative," *New York Times*, February 8, 2006.

10. David Holley, "G-8 Finance Chiefs See Costs of Energy as Threat to Economy," *Los Angeles Times*, in the *San Francisco Chronicle*, February 12, 2006.

11. Robert Collin first reported the story in *Aftonbladet*. For an account in English, see <www.trollhattansaab.net/archives/Saab_hybrid>.

12. "Militants Threaten Flow of Nigerian Oil," *San Francisco Chronicle*, March 6, 2006, 3.

13. Hassan M. Fattah, "Suicide Bomb Attack on Saudi Plant Thwarted," *New York Times*, in the *San Francisco Chronicle*, February 25, 2006.

14. Sam Howe Verhovek, "Oil Spill Estimate Increased for Pipeline Leak in Alaska," *Los Angeles Times*, in the *San Francisco Chronicle*, March 11, 2006.

15. Nader Elhefnawy, "US Army War College on Energy Security," *Parameters* (US Army War College), March 6, 2006, reprinted in *Energy Bulletin*, <www.energybulletin.net/print.php?id=13481>.

16. Donald F. Fournier and Eileen T. Westervelt, "Energy Trends and Their Implications for US Army Installations," US Army Corps of Engineers, Washington, DC, ERDC/CERL TR-05-21, September 2005.

17. Transcript of President Bush's speech at Johnson Controls on the White House website, <www.whitehouse.gov/news/re leases/2006/02/rint/20060220-1.html>.

18. See all the smiling faces on Capitol Hill on the CalCars website. <www.calcars.org/phevs-in-dc.html>.

19. Karl Vick, "Iran Renews Oil Threat Ahead of Possible UN Nuclear Vote," *Washington Post,* in the *San Francisco Chronicle,* March 6, 2006, 3.

20. "Threat of Impasse on Security Council," *San Francisco Chronicle,* March 14, 2006, 3.

Chapter 11

1. Tara Burghart, "Argonne's Drive: New Fuels for Cars," *Chicago Sun-Times,* May 29, 2006.

2. Data from National Renewable Energy Laboratory Study 714209, featured in FreedomCAR and Vehicle Technologies Fact of the Week #377: June 20, 2005, "New Vehicle Purchase Preference," <www.eere.energy.gov/vehiclesandfuels/facts/20 05/fcvt_fotw377.shtml?print>.

3. Dean Taylor, Southern California Edison, "Life Cycle Cost Study Assumptions," presentation at Electric Drive Transportation Association, December 8, 2005.

4. Harris Interactive, Inc., <http://results.hpolsurveys.com/ins tantresults.aspx/j=w17060>.

5. "Alternative-Fueled Vehicles Seriously Considered by One-Third of US Adults Planning to Purchase or Lease a New Vehicle," *Wall Street Journal* Online/Harris Interactive Personal Finance Poll: <www.harrisinteractive.com/news/allnewsbyda te.asp?NewsID=1044>.

6. "Drivers Feel Pressure at the Pumps," *Consumer Reports,* May 2006. <www.consumerreports.org/cro/cars/news/fuel-econo my-survey/overview/p83292.htm>.

7. David Gow, "Ten Years Down the Road: Car Giant Foresees the Non-polluting Accident-proof Saloon," *The Guardian,* March 31, 2006. <www.guardian.co.uk/climatechange/story/ 0,1743810,00.html>.

8. Mike Lindblom, "To Really Save on Gas, Hybrid Car Grows

Tail," *Seattle Times,* June 19, 2006. <http://seattletimes.nw source.com/html/localnews/2003070514_newplugin cars/9m.html>.

9. Associated Press, "Toyota Considers Plug-in Hybrids," in the *Wall Street Journal,* July 18, 2006, <http://online.wsj.com/SB 115323638623409864.html>.

10. Jeff Green, "GM Plans Gas-electric Car, People Say," *Bloomberg News,* June 23, 2006, published in *Chicago Tribune* and other outlets; Chris Isidore, "GM Eyes 'Plug-in' Hybrid," CNNMoney.com, June 23, 2006. <http://cnnmoney/2006/06 /23/news/companies/gm_plugin_hybrid/>.

Index

About the Author

S HERRY BOSCHERT has been an award-winning medical news
reporter in the San Francisco bureau of International Medical News Group, a division of Elsevier, since 1991. A committed
environmentalist, the addition of solar panels to her roof led her
to buy an electric car and to co-founding the San Francisco
Electric Vehicle Association, of which she is President.

If you have enjoyed *Plug-in Hybrids* you might also enjoy other

BOOKS TO BUILD A NEW SOCIETY

Our books provide positive solutions for people who want to
make a difference. We specialize in:

**Environment and Justice • Conscientious Commerce • Sustainable Living
Ecological Design and Planning • Natural Building & Appropriate Technology
New Forestry • Educational and Parenting Resources • Nonviolence
Progressive Leadership • Resistance and Community**

New Society Publishers

ENVIRONMENTAL BENEFITS STATEMENT

New Society Publishers has chosen to produce this book on recycled paper made with
100% post consumer waste, processed chlorine free, and old growth free.

For every 5,000 books printed, New Society saves the following resources:[1]

24	Trees
2,188	Pounds of Solid Waste
2,408	Gallons of Water
3,140	Kilowatt Hours of Electricity
3,978	Pounds of Greenhouse Gases
17	Pounds of HAPs, VOCs, and AOX Combined
7	Cubic Yards of Landfill Space

[1]Environmental benefits are calculated based on research done by the Environmental Defense Fund and
other members of the Paper Task Force who study the environmental impacts of the paper industry.

For a full list of NSP's titles, please call **1-800-567-6772** *or check out our website at:*

www.newsociety.com

NEW SOCIETY PUBLISHERS